WORLD WIDE RECIPES

Presented by
Home Economics Teachers

Edited by
Gerry Murry Henderson

Graphics By
Robert Knies Design, Inc.

©Library of Congress Catalog
Card No. 83-072748
ISBN 0-914159-10-0

©California Cookbook Company
1907 Skycrest Drive, Fullerton, CA 92631

WORLD WIDE RECIPES
Credits and "Thank You's"!
To:

- **Home Economics Teachers of California**, who contributed all the recipes herein
- **Gerry Henderson**, of Temple City High School, our annual editor
- **Nancy Freeman**, our "CCC" office manager
- **Ina Tjio**, our "computer advisor"
- **Doug Herrema**, our Director of Publications, for book titles and photographs
- **Doug Pierce**, for being our Top Salesman for many years
- **Robert Knies**, of Knies Design, Inc., Fullerton, for graphics, art work and cover-design
- **Bob Clemensen** of Associated Typographers, in Anaheim
- **Jerry Bernstein** of KNI, Inc., in Anaheim, for printing, cutting, collating and binding the books
- **Russ Herrema**, my "main man", and Bill Horton and Bill O'Brien, for deliveries and pick-ups all over California
- **You**, the "Reader" and "Purchaser" of this book, as it supports local schools and children, and creates many jobs!

Thank You ALL!

Grady W. Reed, Owner
California Cookbook Company

P.S. PLEASE NOTE THE RE-ORDER FORM ON PAGE 152!

On Our Front Cover:
"Stir-Fried Pork Burritos," recipe on pg. 121
compliments of the National Pork Producers Council

COLOR PHOTOGRAPHY CREDITS
Courtesy of:
National Pork Producers Council, Des Moines, Iowa
National Livestock & Meat Board, Chicago, Ilinois
National Fisheries Institute, Arlington, Virginia
National Broiler Council, Columbia, South Carolina
Del Monte Foods, San Francisco, California
The Pillsbury Company, Minneapolis, Minnesota
California Poultry Industry Federation, Modesto, California
Wisconsin Milk Marketing Board, Madison, Wisconsin
Hershey Foods Corporation, Hershey, Pennsylvania

CONTENTS

CALIFORNIA HOME ECONOMICS TEACHERS ADVISORY COMMITTEE

Banicevich, Gerry
Cordova Sr. High School,
Rancho Cordova

Black-Eaker, Ellen
Nogales High School, La Puente

Carr, Mary
Enterprise High School, Redding

Delap, Carol
Goldenwest High School, Visalia

Drewisch, Carrie
Vandenberg Middle School,
Vandenberg AFB

Estes, Marianne
La Mirada High School, La Mirada

Fecchino, Pam
Cimmaron-Memorial High School
Las Vegas, NV

Ford, Pam
Temecula Valley High School, Temecula

Fregulia, Maria
Lassen High School, Susanville

Geer, Donna, Assistant Principal
Chino High School, Chino

Glennan, Renee
Sequoia Jr. High School, Simi Valley

Grohmann, Joyce
Bellflower High School, Bellflower

Henderson, Gerry
Temple City High School, Temple City

Hibma, Grace, Office of L.A. County
Superintendent of Schools, Consultant
Consumer & Homemaking Education

Himenes, Peggy
Actis Jr. High School, Bakersfield

Hulen, Donna
Los Alamitos High School, Los Alamitos

Jones, Dottie
Etiwanda High School, Etiwanda

Lash, Mary
Paramount High School,
Paramount

Lopez, Karen
San Luis Obispo High School,
San Luis Obispo

Lundy, Jeri
Grossmont High School, La Mesa

Lupul, Darlene
Tokay High School, Lodi

Matsuno, Dale
Bell Gardens High School
Bell Gardens

Pendleton, Susie
Cerritos High School, Cerritos

Priestley, Roberta
Alhambra High School, Alhambra

Ruth, Lynda
La Mirada High School, La Mirada

Sheats, Dianne
Gridley High School, Gridley

Shepherd, Maxine, retired
Moreno Valley High School
Moreno Valley

Shrock, Bonnie
Kearny High School, San Diego

Sweet-Gregory, Jill
Santa Paula High School,
Santa Paula

Traw, Marianne
Ball Jr. High School, Anaheim

Wells, Betty
Oroville High School, Oroville

Whitten, Kathryn P.
Regional Supervisor
Home Economics Education,
Fresno

Wildermuth, Ellie
La Canada High School, La Canada

AFRICA

It is not easy to trace the origins of African cooking, nor is it completely possible to label all the culinary traditions and styles of each uniquely different tribe of peoples as "African" food. Most recipes were not put into writing by the African people until well into the 19th century. Historians have relied on diaries, letters, and journals written by Europeans who had traveled to Africa.

Most African dishes developed according to the availability of different meats, fruits, and vegetables in that particular region. Many traditional dishes include plenty of game meats, such as elephant, leopard, deer, monkey, lion, and bush cow. Popular spices, such as thyme, basil, and mint, were used in African recipes well before they were found in any Western dish.

Some dishes are elaborate and surrounded by ritual, some are convenient meals eaten daily because of the abundance of a particular ingredient in the dish. Whatever the case, food has traditionally united the Africans with the land, their family, tribe, ancestors, and gods. Its meaning went far beyond the mere quieting of hunger pangs. Food, like everything else, is interrelated to the whole of African life.

Africa

SAMOOSAS

Serves 4 - 6   **AFRICA**

1 large onion, finely chopped
1 - 2 cloves garlic, finely chopped
1 teaspoon curry powder
1/2 red or green pepper, finely chopped
   (optional)

cooking oil, for deep frying
1 package won ton skins
1 pound lean ground beef

Saute onions, garlic, curry powder and peppers in a small amount of oil. Add meat to sauteed mixture. Cook meat thoroughly; drain fat. Place a small spoonful of meat mixture in center of won ton skin. Wet edges of won ton with water; fold into triangle; press edges. Deep fry a few samoosas at a time. Turn them over in oil. When samoosas are a light golden brown color, remove and drain on a paper towel.

"Samoosas are good hot or cold. They can be frozen before frying or after frying. This recipe came from a friend who lived in Kenya."

Carolyn Cummings   **Newhart Middle School, Mission Viejo, CA**

AFRICAN PEANUT BALLS

Makes 2 dozen   **AFRICA**

1 1/2 cups peanuts, finely chopped
2 1/2 cups flour
3/4 cup margarine, softened to
   room temperature

1/2 cup powdered sugar
2 tablespoons granulated sugar
2 teaspoons vanilla

Preheat oven to 350 degrees. Chop peanuts in food processor. In a medium mixing bowl, blend peanuts and flour. In another mixing bowl, combine margarine and sugars; mix well. Add vanilla and mix well again. Shape mixture into 1" balls and bake on,, ungreased, cookie sheets for 15 to 18 minutes.

"You may garnish the center of each ball with a whole peanut, if desired. This can be used as an enjoyable snack."

Jannie Parks   **Ramona High School, Riverside, CA**

PEPPER STEAK WITH COCONUT

Serves 8

3 pounds tenderloin steak
1 fresh coconut
4 green peppers
1/2 cup peanut or vegetable oil
1 tabelspoon salt
1 teaspoon black pepper
3 cloves garlic, mashed, or 1 teaspoon
  garlic powder

few drops tabasco sauce
2 tablespoons soy sauce
2 beef bouillon cubes
4 tablespoons cornstarch
1/4 cup dry vermouth

Cut tenderloin into 1/2 inch thick strips. Crack coconut, reserving the water. Remove dark skin with vegetable parer and cut coconut in strips same size as steak strips. Slice peppers in strips same size as steak strips. In a 10 inch skillet combine peanut or vegetable oil with salt, pepper, garlic and tabasco. Saute peppers in the seasoned oil for 2 minutes. Add strips of steak and saute for 2 minutes. Add strips of coconut and saute for 2 minutes, blending mixture together. Add water to the coconut water to make up 2 cups. Bring to a boil. Add soy sauce and bouillon. Dissolve cornstarch in dry vermouth and add to the sauce. Stir over low heat until smooth and thickened to sauce consistency. Pour over the pepper steak.

"This recipe was taken from the 1970 edition of "The African Cookbook" by Citadel Press in New York."

Julie Gibbons   **Chemawa Middle School, Riverside, CA**

AMERICANA

Cajun
California
Canada
Soul Food
Southern U.S.
Southwestern U.S.

Canada and the United States share the same European roots in their cooking. The United States, however, being further south, had a climatic and industrial advantage in the development of their livestock industry which made for more meat-oriented dishes to be served in the United States. On the other hand, fish and game prevail in traditional Canadian dishes.

Aside from the English and French culinary influences, there is also the Indian influence, shown in Americans' love for corn-on-the-cob and Canadians' love of squash pies.

The United States is the true "melting pot" of cooking styles, as well as people. This "assimilation" is also exemplified in the influence of Mexican cooking in the southwestern states.

AMERICANA

FRUIT SLUSH PUNCH

Serves 24

AMERICANA

4 cups sugar
6 cups water
5 bananas
1 (46 ounce) can pineapple juice

1 (6 ounce) can frozen orange juice
1 (6 ounce) can frozen lemonade
2 quarts ginger ale

Heat sugar and water until sugar is dissolved; cool. Blend bananas in blender, add a little of the pineapple juice. Combine banana mixture, remaining pineapple juice, orange juice and lemonade, freeze in 1/2 gallon containers. When ready to use, thaw slightly. Put in punch bowl and add a little ginger ale; mash with a potato masher until slushy. Add remaining ginger ale.

"Great to make ahead and have when needed."

Roberta Priestley   **Alhambra High School, Alhambra, CA**

BEACH PARTY PUNCH

Serves 20 - 30

AMERICANA

1 cup amaretto liqueur
1 cup Southern Comfort
1 cup vodka

1 cup peach schnapps
4 1/2 cups orange juice
4 1/2 cups pineapple juice

Combine all ingredients into a large punch bowl. Stir well. Add lots of crushed ice.

"Delicious!"

Laurie Bleecker   **Chino High School, Chino, CA**

EL PASO JALAPEÑO JELLY

Makes 8 cups

SOUTHWESTERN U.S.

1 3/4 cups vinegar
12 jalapeños, peeled and seeded
1 bell pepper, chopped

6 1/2 cups sugar
6 ounces Certo
2 drops green food coloring

In blender, blend 1/2 cup vinegar and jalapeños; add bell pepper and blend until smooth. In large pan, mix sugar and 1 1/4 cups vinegar. Bring to slow boil and add pepper mixture. Cook 5 minutes at a slow boil. Remove from heat and add Certo and stir until well blended. Add green food coloring.

Note: Can be bottled and sealed or frozen.

CAUTION: Wear rubber gloves while working with jalapeños to keep very hot juices from your skin. (I learned the hard way!)

"This is wonderful served as an appetizer. Spread over a block of softened cream cheese and serve with crackers."

Judy Banks   **Temecula Valley High School, Temecula, CA**

BLACK BEAN & FRESH CORN NACHOS W/TOMATO SALSA

Serves 5 - 6   **SOUTHWESTERN U.S.**

1/2 pound bacon, coarsely chopped
1 medium onion, chopped
1 clove garlic, chopped
2 (15 ounce) cans black beans, reserving
*   1/2 cup liquid*
1 tablespoon distilled white vinegar
2 cups corn kernels, cut from 2 medium-
*   sized ears, yellow or white*

1 1/2 cups jalapeño jack cheese,
*   shredded*
1 (14 ounce) bag blue or yellow corn
*   tortilla chips OR*
12 (7 inch) size warm flour tortillas
thin avocado slices, for garnish
*   (optional)*
fresh cilantro, for garnish (optional)

<u>*tomato salsa*</u>
3 medium-sized ripe yellow or red
*   tomatoes, cored and diced*
1 fresh hot chile, seeded and minced
1/2 cup yellow or red bell pepper, minced

1 tablespoon lime juice
2 teaspoons fresh cilantro, minced
salt, to taste

Step 1: In a 10" to 12" frying pan over medium heat, stir bacon, onion and garlic until bacon is crisp, 8 -10 minutes. Drain and discard fat. Drain black beans, reserving 1/2 cup liquid. Add beans, reserved liquid and vinegar to pan. Coarsely mash beans with spoon; if made ahead, cover and chill up to 1 day. Step 2: Prepare salsa by mixing tomato with chili , bell pepper, lime juice, cilantro and salt. Serve, or cover and let stand up to 6 hours. Step 3: Spoon black beans onto a 10" x 13" pan; spread level into about a 10" long oval. Top beans with corn, then cover with cheese. Bake, uncovered, in a 400 degree oven until hot in center, about 10 minutes. Remove from oven and serve with chips or place rolled flour tortillas beside beans. Garnish with avocado or cilantro. Spoon onto plates and top with some salsa. Scoop onto chips or roll into tortillas.

"This is a family favorite. It was also a big hit at the first faculty gathering for the new Scripps Ranch High School."

Bonnie Kau   **Scripps Ranch High School, San Diego, CA**

SAN ANTONIO STYLE CHICKEN WINGS

Serves 24   **SOUTHWESTERN U.S.**

24 chicken wings
1 cup "Pace" picante sauce
1/3 cup catsup

1/4 cup honey
1/4 teaspoon ground cumin

Cut wings in half at joint and discard the tips. Combinell of the ingredients and pour over the chicken. Refrigerate at least 1 hour, turning once. Place chicken on broiler pan and bake at 375 degrees for 30 minutes. Brush chicken with reserved marinade; turn and bake, brushing generously with marinade every 10 minutes, until tender (about 30 minutes). Place about 6 inches from preheated broiler for about 3 minutes until sauce looks dry. Turn over and do the other side.

"A delicious appetizer to spice up any party. This recipe was contributed by Tracey Briggs."

Carrie Drewisch   **Vandenberg Middle School, Lompoc, CA**

TEX-MEX WON TONS

Makes 48   **AMERICANA**

1/2 pound ground beef
1/4 cup onion, chopped
2 tablespoons green pepper, chopped
1/2 (15 ounce) can refried beans
1/4 cup cheddar cheese, shredded
1 tablespoon catsup

1 1/2 teaspoon chili powder
1/4 teaspoon ground cumin
4 dozen won ton skins
oil for deep frying
salsa

Cook ground beef, onion and green pepper in large skillet until meat is brown; drain fat. Stir beans, cheese, catsup, chili powder and cumin into meat mixture. Place won ton skin with one point toward you. Spoon heaping teaspoon of meat mixture into center of skin. Fold bottom point of skin over filling; tuck point under filling. Fold side corners over, forming an envelope shape. Roll up toward remaining corner; moisten point and press to seal. Repeat with remaining skins and filling. Fry a few at a time in oil hot (heated to 375 degrees) about 1 minute per side. Use a slotted spoon to remove won tons; drain. Serve warm with salsa.

"These freeze well and can be reheated; loosely cover with foil in 350 degree oven for 10 to 12 minutes."

Paula Skrifvars   **Brea Junior High School, Brea, CA**

CELERY SEED BREAD

Serves 4   **AMERICANA**

6 tablespoons butter or margarine,
   softened
1/2 teaspoon celery seed

1/4 teaspoon paprika
1/4 teaspoon dried parsley flakes
4 hot dog rolls, sliced

In a mixing bowl, combine butter, celery seed, paprika and parsley flakes, stirring well to blend. Spread on cut sides of each roll. Place on baking sheet; broil until golden brown.

Myrna Westmoreland   **Grace Davis High School, Modesto, CA**

HOWELL'S BREAD

Serves 6 - 8   SOUTHWESTERN U.S.

1 loaf sourdough French bread
1/4 cup butter or margarine, softened to
   room temperature
1 cup green chilies, chopped

garlic powder, to taste
1/2 pound cheddar cheese, grated
1 cup mayonnaise
paprika

Mix butter, chilies and garlic together in a small bowl. Slice the bread lengthwise. Spread
with butter mixture. Blend cheese and mayonnaise. Spread on top. Sprinkle with paprika.
Place on foil under broiler until brown and bubbly.

"Guests will rave about this one!"

Carol Fleming   Rancho Cucamonga High School, Rancho Cucamonga, CA

REAL SOUTHERN CORN BREAD

Serves 4   SOUL FOOD

1 cup corn meal
1/4 cup wheat flour
1/2 teaspoon salt

1/2 cup milk
1 egg, beaten
1 tablespoon butter, melted

Combine the dry ingredients. Combine the milk with beaten egg and add to the dry
ingredients. Add the melted butter and pour batter into a well greased pan. Bake in a hot
oven, 425 degrees, for about 25 minutes.

*"Corn bread is considered 'Soul Food'. But soul food is not exclusively black. All
southerners had an important share in it's development, including soldiers,
explorers, settlers, traders and others of varied nationalities."*

Evelyn Thomas   **Chaffey High School, Ontario, CA**

SOUTHERN BLUEBERRY FRITTERS

Makes 2 dozen   SOUTHERN U.S.

1 cup pancake mix
1/2 cup milk
1 egg, beaten
1/2 teaspoon vanilla

1 cup blueberries, rinsed and drained
oil for deep frying
powdered sugar

In bowl, combine pancake mix, milk, egg and vanilla. Stir until smooth. Lightly stir in
blueberries. Let stand 5 minutes. Drop batter by teaspoonfuls into oil preheated to 375
degrees. Fry about 1 1/2 minutes per side, turning when brown on underside. Drain on
paper towels. Sprinkle with powdered sugar.

Jeri Lane   **Canyon Springs High School, Moreno Valley, CA**

INDIAN FRY BREAD

Serves 4

2 cups flour
1/2 cup instant nonfat dry milk
1 tablespoon baking powder
1/2 teaspoon salt

2 tablespoons shortening
3/4 cup water
oil for frying

Mix together flour, dry milk, baking powder and salt. Cut in 2 tablespoons shortening. Rub mixture with fingers until coarse crumbs form. Add water and stir with a fork until dough clings together. Knead until smooth, 2 to 3 minutes. Break off pieces of dough and form flat circles about 1/4 inch thick. Place into fry pan containing oil heated to 375 degrees. Turning once, cook each round of dough in oil until puffy and golden.

"Shirley Rhoan Forga shared her recipe with our kids. They enjoyed making fry bread and especially eating it. Shirley is a descendant of the Mariposa Miwok and Yosemite Indians."

Judith Huffman   **Mariposa County High School, Mariposa, CA**

SOURDOUGH PANCAKES

Serves 6

starter:
1/2 tablespoon yeast
1 1/2 tablespoons warm water

2 cups buttermilk
1 cup flour

pancakes:
2 cups flour
2 cups milk
1/2 cup starter
2 eggs, beaten

3 tablespoons butter, melted
3 tablespoons sugar
1 1/2 teaspoons baking soda
1 teaspoon salt

Starter: Dissolve yeast in warm water. Add buttermilk and flour. Let stand at room temperature overnight. Next day, refrigerate starter (up to 3 weeks).

Pancakes: Night before - mix flour, milk and 1/2 cup starter. Set in a draft-free place. Let stand overnight. In the morning, combine eggs, melted butter, sugar, baking soda and salt into mixture left overnight. Bake on lightly greased griddle, on medium heat for 2 to 4 minutes.

"My grandpa used to make us sourdough pancakes. He was a sheep rancher and did them the old fashioned way...right in the bag of flour!"

Kristine Haas   **La Habra High School, La Habra, CA**

SUPER BOWL SEAFOOD CHOWDER

Serves 6

2 large onions, chopped
3 tablespoons butter or margarine
1 pound cod fillets (frozen)
1 (10 ounce) package frozen peas
2 cups water
2 teaspoons salt
1 teaspoon pepper

1//2 teaspoons thyme leaves (crumbled)
1 (5 ounce) can lobster meat or small
   shrimp
2 (10 ounce) cans clams
1 can creamed corn
1 can evaporated milk
parsley for garnish

Saute onions in butter or margarine; add cod, peas, water and spices. Cover and heat to a boil; reduce to a simmer and break cod into large flakes. Add lobster, clams, corn and evaporated milk. Cover and heat slowly, just to boiling. Ladle into heated soup bowls and top with chopped parsley.

"A real meal when served with garlic bread. A family favorite for New Year's Day and Super Bowl Sunday! Enjoy!"

Michele Beutler   **A.B. Miller High School, Fontana, CA**

PHYLLIS' COLESLAW

Serves 8 - 10

1 head cabbage, shredded
1/2 quart mayonnaise
1/2 cup evaporated milk
1/4 cup apple cider vinegar

1/4 cup sugar
garlic salt, to taste
onion salt, to taste
pepper, to taste

Mix mayonnaise, evaporated milk, vinegar and spices together. Add cabbage. Mix well and enjoy!

Note: A food processor works really well in shredding cabbage.

"This is an easy recipe to make. My family loves it, and so there are never any leftovers!"

Jeri Lane   **Canyon Springs High School, Moreno Valley, CA**

HOT MACARONI SALAD

Serves 12

2 cups small shell macaroni, uncooked
1 can cream of mushroom soup
1/2 cup milk
1 medium onion, chopped
1/4 cup green pepper, chopped

1/4 cup pimento, drained and chopped
1/2 cup mayonnaise
1 cup cheddar cheese, grated
salt & pepper to taste

Cook macaroni and drain. Blend all ingredients. Pour into a buttered 9" x 13" baking dish. Bake at 400 degrees for 30 minutes.

"This tasty side dish recipe was sent to me by my husband's grandmother in Kansas. It has been a 'hit' at many pot luck suppers."

Sally Reimers   **Charles Jones Junior High School, Baldwin Park, CA**

SOUTHWEST SALAD W/CRISP RED CALIFORNIA CHILES

Serves 6 to 8   SOUTHWESTERN U.S.

1 1/4 pounds (3 -4 quarts) fresh
  salad greens (spinach optional)
6 dried California chiles
1/4 cup olive or salad oil
2/3 cup cider vinegar
1 clove garlic, minced or pressed
1 tablespoon soy sauce

1/4 teaspoon pepper, freshly ground
2 large, ripe avocados
1 pound asadero (Mexican style string
  cheese) or mozzarella, cut into
  1/2 inch cubes
1 large red onion, thinly sliced

Wash, dry greens. Wrap in paper towels, enclose in plastic bag, refrigerate 30 minutes (up to 2 days).With scissors, cut chiles crosswise into thin strips, discard stems and seeds. In a wide frying pan, over low heat, stir oil and chiles until chiles are crisp (2 to 3 minutes). Watch closely to avoid burning. Lift chiles from oil; set aside. Save oil for dressing.

To prepare Cider Dressing: mix oil from chiles with cider vinegar, garlic, soy sauce and pepper, whisk well.When ready to serve, tear greens into bite-sized pieces. Add avocados, cheese, onion and toasted chiles. Toss with Cider Dressing.

Sally Paul   **Winters High School, Winters, CA**

SUMMER STYLE BAKED BEANS

Serves 4 - 6   AMERICANA

1/4 cup molasses
1 tablespoon prepared mustard
1 tablespoon vinegar

2 (1 pound) cans B&M baked beans
1 tomato, sliced
1 onion, sliced

Mix together molasses, mustard and vinegar. Stir into beans which have been placed in a heavy skillet. Place skillet on outdoor grill in a warm spot. Heat slowly to serving temperature while grilling meat or other foods.

"Easy and good."

Gage Hewes   **South Pasadena High School, South Pasadena, CA**

GREENS WITH SMOKED HAM HOCKS

Serves 8 - 10   SOUL FOOD

2 smoked ham hocks
1 1/2 quarts water
1 to 2 hot pepper pods or 1 teaspoon
  crushed red pepper
3 cloves garlic, crushed

4 pounds fresh collard, turnips, kale or
  mustard greens (or mixture)
1 teaspoon sugar
salt to taste

Place ham hocks in Dutch oven or large saucepan; add water, pepper pods and garlic. Cover. Bring to boil; reduce heat and simmer 2 hours or until hocks are tender. Break off stems of greens. Wash leaves thoroughly. Slice leaves into bite-size pieces by rolling several leaves together and slicing in 1/4 inch strips. Add greens, sugar and salt to hocks. Cook 30 to 40 minutes, or until greens are done.

"This recipe comes from an Ebony Magazine article entitled 'Soul Food For All'"

Inez Roberson   **Correia Junior High School, San Diego, CA**

CANDIED YAMS

Serves 8   **SOUTHERN U.S.**

3 - 4 medium yams   *1/3 cup vinegar*
3/4 brown sugar   *cinnamon*
3/4 cup granulated sugar   *margarine*
1 cup water

Cook yams in water until fork tender. Peel, Slice lengthwise about 3/4 inch thick. Arrange yams in a 9" x 13" glass utility dish. Mix sugars and water in small saucepan. Cook to boiling, simmer until syrupy (about 1/2 hour). Add vinegar (do not boil after adding). Pour syrup over yams. Sprinkle with cinnamon and dot with margarine. Bake at 350 degrees for 30 to 45 minutes, basting frequently.

"This recipe is a family favorite my grandmother brought from Alabama."

Carolyn McBride   **Arcadia High School, Arcadia, CA**

CHICKEN STROGANOFF

Serves 8   **AMERICANA**

8 chicken breasts, boned and skinned   *1/2 teaspoon paprika*
1 (16 ounce) carton sour cream   *1/2 teaspoon garlic salt*
1 can cream of mushroom soup   *1/2 teaspoon onion salt*
2 cups flour   *2 cups sharp cheddar cheese, shredded*
2 teaspoons salt   *oil for frying*
1/4 teaspoon pepper   *cooked rice*

Mix sour cream and soup together, set aside. Place flour and all seasonings together in a small paper bag. Toss each piece of chicken in flour mixture. Brown chicken in hot oil. Place browned chicken in a 9" x 13" casserole dish. Top chicken with soup mixture and bake at 350 degrees for 45 minutes. Top with cheese during last 15 minutes of baking. Serve with rice.

"Thanks to my sister for this winning recipe. It has been a success each time served. Great buffet dish."

Carol Goddard   **Alhambra High School, Alhambra, CA**

CAJUN CHICKEN BROCHETTES

Serves 6   SOUTHERN U.S.

1/2 small onion
1 medium clove garlic
1/4 cup safflower oil
1 tablespoon fresh lime juice
2 teaspoons Hungarian paprika
1 teaspoon ground oregano
1 teaspoon dried thyme, crumbled

1/4 teaspoon cayenne pepper
6 chicken breasts or thighs, skinned &
*   deboned, cut into chunks*
1 large onion
2 limes, scored lenthwise
12 medium mushrooms
12 cherry tomatoes

Combine 1/2 small onion, garlic, oil, lime juice, Hungarian paprika, oregano, thyme and cayenne pepper and grind in a food processor. Transfer to a resealable plastic bag. Add skinned and boned chicken and seal bag. Refrigerate 4 hours or overnight.

Cut large onion into 12 1-1/2" squares. Place on brochette alternating chicken with lime, onion, mushrooms, tomatoes. Place 6" from heat, cook 10 to 12 minutes, or until chicken is opaque.

Maria Hoffman   **Katella High School, Anaheim, CA**

SOUTHERN CHICKEN CASSEROLE

Serves 8 - 10   SOUTHERN U.S.

2 cups cooked chicken, chopped
2 cups cooked rice, cooled
2 cups celery, chopped
4 tablespoon onion, chopped
2 cans condensed cream of chicken soup

2 cups water chestnuts, sliced
1 1/2 cups mayonnaise
1 package Stove Top stuffing
3 ounces butter or margarine, melted

Mix together the first 7 seven ingredients. Place in a casserole dish. Top with dry Stove Top stuffing (discard seasoning packet). Drizzle butter over top and bake at 350 degrees for 45 minutes.

"Everyone likes it—great for making the night before!"
Margaret McLeod   **Nogales High School, La Puente, CA**

CALIFORNIA SNAPPER

Serves 8   CALIFORNIA

1 (16 ounce) can green enchilada sauce
2 pounds red snapper fillets
1/2 onion, chopped

jack cheese, grated
1 large tomato, diced
1 avocado, sliced

Spray a 13" x 9" baking dish with non-stick cooking spray. Pour some of the enchilada sauce into the pan and lay fillets leaving space in between (this makes it easier to remove). Cover with remainder of sauce and top with chopped onions. Cook for 12 minutes at 325 degrees. Sprinkle grated cheese over fillets and bake for 3 minutes more. Place fillets on plates and pour extra sauce over, if desired. Sprinkle with diced tomatoes and decorate with slices of avocado.

Donna Love   **Pinon Mesa Middle School, Phelan, CA**

HOT 'N SPICY BEEF BACK RIBS

Serves 8 - 10   **SOUL FOOD**

7 pounds beef back ribs
3/4 cup water, divided
1 cup catsup
2 tablespoons fresh lemon juice

1 teaspoon ground cinnamon
1 teaspoon hot pepper sauce
1/2 to 1 teaspoon crushed red
*   pepper pods*

Place each beef back ribs rack, meat side down, in center of double-thick rectangle of heavy duty aluminum foil (twice the length of the slab plus 8 inches). Sprinkle 2 tablespoons water over ribs. To form packets, bring two opposite sides of aluminum foil together over top of ribs. Fold edges over 3 to 4 times pressing crease in tightly each time (allow some air space). Flatten aluminum foil at both ends; crease to form triangle and fold each end over several times toward packet, pressing tightly to seal. Place packets on grid over low to medium coals. Place cover on cooker and grill 1½ hours, turning packets every ½ hour. Meanwhile, combine catsup, remaining ½ cup water, lemon juice, cinnamon, pepper sauce and pepper pods in a small saucepan. Bring to a boil; reduce heat. Cook slowly 10-12 minutes, stirring occasionally. Remove ribs from packets; place on grid over medium coals.* Grill 30-40 minutes, turning and brushing with sauce occasionally. Serve ribs with remaining sauce.
*To check temperature, cautiously hold hand about 4 inches above coals. Low to medium coals will force removal of hand in 4 to 5 seconds.
NOTE: Ribs may also be cooked on an open cooker. Prepare beef back ribs in aluminum foil packets and place on grid over medium coals* as directed above. Increase cooking time to 2 hours, turning packets every ½ hour. Continue with remaining procedures as directed.

National Live Stock & Meat Board   **Chicago, IL**

STUFFED FRENCH BREAD

Serves 4 - 6   **AMERICANA**

16 slices bread, cubed
2 (8 ounce) packages cream cheese
12 eggs
2 cups milk

1/3 cup maple syrup
powdered sugar
fresh strawberries (optional)

In a casserole dish, alternately layer bread cubes and cream cheese. Combine eggs and milk and beat well. Pour over bread/cream cheese mixture and bake at 350 degrees for 45 minutes. Top with warmed maple syrup and powdered sugar. Fresh strawberries go great with this.

"My family enjoys this for breakfast on Sundays. I like it because while it's baking, I can clean up the mess. It's great!"

Linda Brayton   **Grace Davis High School, Modesto, CA**

CANADIAN CABBAGE ROLLS

Serves 8 - 10   CANADA

1 cup white rice	2 medium yellow onions
1/4 cup barley	2 - 3 cloves garlic, crushed
2 cups water	1 teaspoon pepper
1/2 pound salt pork	1 head green cabbage

Steam rice and barley together with water for 15 minutes; set aside. Cube salt pork; fry and drain drippings. Add diced onions and crushed garlic to drained salt pork; saute until onions are tender. Add steamed rice, barley and pepper blending together; set aside. Separate cabbage leaves and wilt in steaming water 2 - 3 minutes, until bendable. Place 1 tablespoon of filling at one end of leaf and roll up as a small burritos. Place in greased casserole - top with left over leaves to keep moist. Bake, covered or uncovered, at 350 degrees for 45 minutes.

"A traditional Christmas dish - and enjoyed several times during the year."
Darlene Lupul   **Tokay High School, Lodi, CA**

BARBECUED MEATBALLS

Serves 5   SOUTHWESTERN U.S.

Meatballs:	*Sauce:*
2/3 cup undiluted canned milk	1 (16 ounce) jar Welch's grape jelly
1 1/2 pounds lean ground beef	1 (16 ounce) bottle barbeque sauce
1/2 cup onion, finely chopped	
2/3 cup cracker crumbs	
1 teaspoon salt	

Combine meatball ingredients and form into 1 inch balls. Place on foil-lined cookie sheets and bake at 400 degrees for 20 to 30 minutes, or until done. Combine grape jelly and barbecue sauce in a saucepan or crockpot and stir until mixed well. Add meatballs and heat thoroughly. Serve with rice or noodles or alone.

"Handed down from my grandmother and mother from Texas and they are a favorite! This can also be doubled for a large crowd."
Jean Mornac   **Hillside Junior High School, Simi Valley, CA**

RING AROUND MEATBALLS

Serves 6   AMERICANA

1 can mushrooms	1 tesapoon salt
milk (less than 1/2 cup)	1/8 teaspoon pepper
1 pound ground beef	1 egg, beaten
3/4 cup soft bread crumbs	2 large green bell peppers
2 tablespoons onion, chopped	2 tablespoons catsup
1 teaspoon worcestershire sauce	2 tablespoons grated cheese

Drain mushrooms; reserve liquid. Add enough milk to liquid to make 1/2 cup liquid. Combine ground beef, mushrooms, liquid, bread crumbs, onion, worcestershire sauce, salt, pepper and egg. Clean bell peppers; cut into 6" rings. Place rings in a shallow baking pan. Make 6 large meatballs and pack into rings. Bake at 350 degrees for 35 minutes. Combine catsup and grated cheese and spoon over meatballs. Continue baking for 10 more minutes.

Julie Carriere   North Monterey County High School, Castroville, CA

CHILI BOWLS

Serves 4   **SOUTHWESTERN U.S.**

*1 pound loaf frozen bread dough
    (I use Bridgford)
2 tablespoons butter, melted
1 onion, chopped
1 pound hamburger
2 cans tomato soup
2 cups pinto or kidney beans,
    including liquid
1/2 cup water*

*2 tablespoons chili powder (or more
    to taste)
1/2 teaspoon salt
1/4 teaspoon pepper
1/4 teaspoon cayenne pepper (or
    more to taste if you want it hotter)
cheese, shredded (for topping)
onions, chopped (for topping)*

Thaw bread dough. When soft enough, cut loaf crosswise into 4 pieces. Shape into balls. Place balls 3 inches apart on lightly greased cookie sheet. Brush with melted butter. Let rise, approximately 1 hour. Bake at 375 degrees for 20 to 25 minutes or until golden brown. Remove from pan immediately to cool on rack. To make into chili bowls, slice off tops of bowls and hollow out by pinching bread out with fingers. Toast bowl by placing in oven or under broiler. Set aside.

Brown onion and hamburger in frying pan. When brown, drain grease; then add soup, beans, water, chili powder, salt, pepper and cayenne pepper. Cook on low heat for an hour or more (or less)When ready to serve, fill chili "bowls" with chili; top with grated cheese and/or chopped onion.

"I received this recipe from Bridgford Bread. My students and my family both like it. If you are in a hurry, bake the bowls and fill with canned chili."

Gloria King   Schurr High School, Montebello, CA

CAMPER'S STEW

Serves 8 - 10   **SOUTHWESTERN U.S.**

*1 pound bacon
1 large onion, chopped
2 cans tomatoes (may be blended)*

*2 cans beans, undrained
1 small box quick brown rice*

Brown the bacon; remove from pan and break into bits. Saute the onion in bacon fat. Drain excess fat. Add canned tomatoes, beans and 2 cans water and rice. Simmer until rice is cooked. Serve with biscuits.

"This recipe comes from my mother-in-law, Gail Folsom, and was originally prepared in a cast iron pot over the campfire. Now, we fix it in the motorhome and eat it around the campfire. An old family tradition."

Joan Goodell   Eldorado High School, Las Vegas, NV

BRUNSWICK STEW

Serves 12

1 large (4 pound) chicken
4 cups cold water
1 (5 to 6 pound) pork roast, Boston
*   butt if possible*
2 (16 ounce) cans tomatoes, chopped
4 cups corn, fresh or canned
1 onion, diced
3 potatoes, diced
4 cups small lima beans, canned or frozen

2 cups okra, sliced (optional)
1/2 cup butter
3 tablespoons vinegar
1 tablespoon sugar
2 teaspoons salt
1 teaspoon pepper
1 tablespoon worcestershire sauce
tabasco sauce, few drops at a time

Simmer chicken in water for 1 hour or until tender; cool and remove meat from bones, reserving broth. Bake pork roast at 325 degrees until done. Shred chicken and pork and place in a large heavy pot. Add reserved chicken broth, all vegetables, butter, vinegar and sugar; simmer 6 to 8 hours until thickened. As stew thickens season to taste with salt, pepper, worcestershire and tabasco. The secret to this stew is the long, slow simmering.

"This stew is claimed to have originated in Brunswick, Georgia. It was always served at large southern barbecues along with slices of white bread and butter. I request this when I go to Georgia for a visit, since I have never found this on a menu in California."

Alice Lewandowski   **Linden High School, Linden, CA**

SOUTHWEST CHICKEN BREASTS

Serves 4

1/3 cup olive oil
2 limes, juice only
1/4 cup balsamic vinegar
1 teaspoon dijon mustard
2 cloves garlic, crushed

1/4 cup cilantro, chopped
1/2 teaspoon salt
1/2 teaspoon pepper
4 chicken breasts, boneless, skinless

Combine oil, lime juice, balsamic vinegar, dijon mustard, garlic, cilantro, salt and pepper in a bowl. Marinate chicken at least 1 hour. Grill or broil chicken breasts until done, basting with marinade.

NOTE: Fish may be substituted for chicken.

"Served with fresh salad, rice and sourdough bread, this makes a delicious meal."

Wendy Johnson   **Temecula Valley High School, Temecula, CA**

CHICKEN SONORA

Serves 6 - 8

Seasoning mixture:
1 large onion, sliced
3 cloves garlic, peeled
1 inch piece ginger root (do not
*   substitute ground)*

1 teaspoon salt
1/4 teaspoon cayenne pepper
juice of 1 lime
1/4 cup butter, melted

4 whole chicken breasts, boned, but not skinned
12 to 16 flour tortillas, buttered on one side, stacked, wrapped in foil

SEASONED SOUR CREAM MIXTURE:

1 cup sour cream
1/2 teaspoon salt

1/2 teaspoon ground cumin
2 teaspoons fresh cilantro, finely chopped

VEGETABLE GARNISH:

2 - 3 large ripe tomatoes, halved and
  thinly sliced
1 to 2 cucumbers, peeled, quartered
  lengthwise, thinly sliced
1 large bunch green onions, sliced
  (including tops)

1 large ripe avocado, sliced in crescents
2 tablespoons olive oil
juice of 1 lime
salt
freshly ground black pepper

Preheat oven to 350 degrees. In a blender, combine seasoning mixture ingredients. Blend until smooth. Rinse and dry chicken breasts. Dip the chicken pieces into the seasoning mixture to coat. Place chicken, skin side up, in a shallow baking dish. Pour any remaining seasoning mixture over the breasts. Bake, uncovered 45 minutes to 1 hour. Chicken should be nicely browned, but not dried out. During last 20 minutes of baking time, place wrapped tortillas in oven alongside the chicken and heat through.

Meanwhile, combine sour cream, salt, cumin and cilantro in a serving bowl and refrigerate to allow flavors to blend while chicken in baking. Arrange the vegetable garnishes on a serving platter and sprinkle with olive oil, lime juice, salt and pepper.

Just before serving, cut cooked chicken into strips.

To serve: onto a hot tortilla, spoon some chicken, vegetables and seasoned sour cream. Roll up the tortilla. Do not overfill or tortilla will tear when rolled. Serve with a simple rice pilaf.

Note: Much of this dish can be prepared ahead, but bake the chicken at the last minute.

"A delicious 'twist 'on the traditional burrito. I serve these at Southwestern parties with rice pilaf and a fancy dessert."

Luann Goedert　　　　　　　　　　**Carlsbad High School, Carlsbad, CA**

SOUR CREAM ENCHILADAS

Serves 8　　　　　　　　　　　　　　　　**SOUTHWESTERN** U.S.

3/4 pound hamburger
1/2 medium onion, chopped
1 teaspoon garlic
1 (16 ounce) carton sour cream
1 can cream of chicken soup

2 cups cheddar cheese, grated
vegetable cooking spray
8 small - medium tortillas
16 black olives, sliced (optional)

Brown hamburger; drain excess fat. Add onion and garlic and cook until soft; set aside. In a saucepan, mix sour cream, cream of chicken soup and 1 cup cheese. (Remove 3/4 cup of mixture and set aside.) Mix remaining mixture with meat mixture. Spray 11 3/4" x 7 1/2" x 1 3/4" glass baking dish with cooking spray. Fill each tortilla with 1/4 to 1/2 cup filling and roll. Place in pan, seam side down. Spread reserved 3/4 cup sour cream mixture over tortillas, covering all of them. Sprinkle with 1 cup remaining cheese and top with olives. Bake at 350 degrees for 35 minutes.

"You can make this recipe low-fat by substituting ground turkey for hamburger, non-fat cheese, and sour cream, etc."

Teresa Stahl   **Needles Middle/High School, Needles, CA**

ALMOND ROCA (OR ALMOND CHOCOLATE BARK)

Makes 1 1/2 pounds   AMERICANA

1 cup sugar
1 cup butter
1 cup almonds, coarsely chopped

1 (12 ounce)package milk chocolate
   chips (semi-sweet is okay)

In a 2 quart saucepan, mix together sugar and butter. Over medium-high to high heat, cook mixture, stirring constantly to keep butter and sugar from separating. Continue cooking until mixture is "blond-brown", but NOT dark brown. (Mixture will start pulling away from sides of pan.) Remove from heat and quickly stir in almonds. Spread out quite thin (1/4 inch) on greased cookie sheet. Place 1 cup milk chocolate chips over candy mass, spreading when it melts. Place in freezer until chilled and chocolate is hardened (20 to 30 minutes). Remove from freezer, turning whole candy mass over (lift up whole piece) and spread equal amount of melted milk chocolate on other side. Melt chocolate for one minute in microwave to make it spreadable. Freeze again until set. Break apart and enjoy! May be stored in freezer, refrigerator in closed container or at room temperature (under 70 degrees).

"Delicious candy made by my friend's mom when I'd spend the summer in Chico in the late 50's, early 60's."

Carla Escola   **Ripon High School, Ripon, CA**

VACUUM CLEANER COOKIE BARS

Makes 2 dozen   AMERICANA

1/2 cup margarine, melted (do not
   use butter)
1 (18.25 ounce) box yellow cake mix
   (no pudding in batter)
3 eggs

1 (8 ounce) package cream cheese,
   softened
1 (1 pound) box powdered sugar
1/2 cup coconut, flaked
1/2 cup walnuts, chopped

Combine margarine, cake mix and 1 egg. Stir together until dry ingredients are moistened. Pat mixture into bottom of well greased 9" x 13" pan. Beat remaining 2 eggs slightly, then beat in cream cheese and powdered sugar. Stir in coconut and nuts. Pour over mixture in pan, spreading evenly. Bake at 325 degrees for 45 - 50 minutes or until golden brown. Cool pan on wire rack to room temperature before slicing.

"The recipe for this yummy treat was shared with me by a student, Danielle Erwin."

Rhonda Nelson   **Warren High School, Downey, CA**

THE ORIGINAL SONORA FRUIT TACO

Serves 16   CALIFORNIA

1/2 pound almonds, toasted   1 whole mango, peeled and sliced
1/2 pound sugar   1 kiwi, peeled and sliced
3 ounces flour   4 strawberries, sliced
1 ounce cocoa powder   1 peach, sliced
8 egg whites   1/2 cup raspberries
1 whole egg   1/2 cup blackberries
2 ounces butter, browned (imparts   mint leaves for garnish
   hazelnut flavor)

Mix almonds, sugar, flour and cocoa powder together. Add egg whites and whole egg. Brown butter in skillet, being careful to keep it from burning. Add to egg mixture. Mix well. Spray a sheet pan with non-stick cooking spray. Drop by tablespoons onto pan, keeping 6 inches between cookies. With back of spoon, pound out batter to form 4" circles. Bake at 350 degrees for 5 minutes. Put hot baked cookies in a small glass to shape like a taco. Once cooled, cookies cannot be molded to shape so do this immediately. Set aside to cool. Combine fresh fruit and fill taco "cookie".

Carole Call   **Costa Mesa High School, Costa Mesa, CA**

APPLE NUT LATTICE TART

Serves 8   AMERICANA

1 (15 ounce) package Pillsbury   1 teaspoon flour
   All Ready Pie Crusts

Filling:
3 to 3 1/2 cups apples, peeled and 1/2 teaspoon cinnamon
   thinly sliced   1/4 to 1/2 teaspoon lemon peel, grated
1/2 cup sugar   2 teaspoons lemon juice
3 tablespoons golden raisins   1 egg yolk, beaten
3 tablespoons walnuts or pecans,   1 teaspoon water
   chopped

Glaze:
1/4 cup powdered sugar   1 - 2 teaspoons lemon juice

Heat oven to 400 degrees. Prepare pie crust according to package directions for two-crust pie; using 10" tart pan with removable bottom or 9" pie pan. Place 1 prepared crust in pan; press in bottom and up sides of pan. Trim edges if necessary. In a large bowl, combine apples, sugar, raisins, walnuts, cinnamon, lemon peel and lemon juice. Spoon into pie crust lined pan. To make a lattice top, cut remaining crust into 1/2 inch wide strips. Arrange strips in lattice design over apple mixture. Trim and seal edges. Cool for 1 hour. In small bowl, combine egg yolk and water; gently brush over lattice. Bake for 40 to 60 minutes, or until golden brown and apples are tender. In small bowl, combine glaze ingredients and drizzle over slightly warm tart. Cool; remove sides of pan to serve.

NOTE: Cover pie with foil during last 15 to 20 minutes of baking if necessary to prevent excessive browning.

The Pillsbury Company   Minneapolis, MN

MISSION IMPOSSIBLE PIE

Serves 16   AMERICANA

4 eggs   1/2 cup self-rising flour
1/4 cup margarine, melted   2 cups milk
1 3/4 cup sugar   1/2 cup coconut

Beat eggs thoroughly. Add margarine, sugar, flour and milk. Beat until well mixed. Stir in coconut. Pour into 2 ungreased 8" pie pans. Bake at 350 degrees for 35 to 40 minutes. Cool before serving.

NOTE: Do not use a pie crust, this pie makes it's own top and bottom. The mixture is rather thin when poured into pans, but after baking, it cuts clean.

"My mom, Rosemarie Stephens, has many great recipes in her collection. This is a simple and fun one that is very tasty."

Linda Heinbach   Yosemite High School, Oakhurst, CA

STRAWBERRY GLAZED CHEESE PIE

Serves 8   AMERICANA

1 8-inch baked pie shell   2 tablespoon orange juice
1 (8 ounce) package cream cheese, at   2 tablespoons light cream
    room temperature   2 pints fresh strawberries, washed
1 1/3 cups sugar, divided   gently and drained
1 teaspoon grated orange peel   2 tablespoons cornstarch

Beat cream cheese, 1/3 cup sugar, orange peel, orange juice and light cream until mixture is light and fluffy. Spread mixture in baked, cooled pie shell. Place one pint of whole strawberries over cream cheese mixture. Crushed the remaining pint of strawberries Place strawberries, 1 cup sugar and 2 tablespoons cornstarch in a saucepan and cook until translucent and thickened. Pour cooled glaze over berries in pie shell. Refrigerate until chilled, about 3 hours.

Nan Paul   Grant Middle School, Escondido, CA

GREENIE'S SWEET POTATO PIE

Serves 6 - 8   SOUL FOOD

Pastry for 9" one crust pie   1/4 cup butter or margarine
3/4 cup sugar   1 egg, slightly beaten
1 tablespoon all-purpose flour   1 tablespoon lemon juice
1/2 teaspoon baking powder   1 teaspoon vanilla extract
1/2 teaspoon ground nutmeg   1 1/4 cups milk or evaporated milk
2 cups sweet potatoes, hot & cooked
    (about 2 medium potatoes)

Heat oven to 425 degrees. Prepare pastry. Combine sugar, flour, baking powder and nutmeg in medium mixer bowl; add remaining ingredients and beat until well blended. Place pastry-lined pie plate on oven rack; pour in filling. Bake 15 minutes. Reduce oven temperature to 350 degrees. Bake until knife inserted in center comes out clean, about 45 minutes longer.

"This recipe comes from an Ebony Magazine article entitled 'Soul Food for All'"
Inez Roberson   **Correia Junior High School, San Diego, CA**

TEXAS SHEET CAKE

Serves 24   **SOUTHWESTERN U.S.**

Cake:
2 cups sugar
2 cups flour
1/2 cup margarine
3 heaping tablespoons cocoa
1 cup water

1/2 cup shortening
1/2 cup buttermilk
2 eggs
1 teaspoon baking soda
1 tablespoon vanilla

Frosting:
1/2 cup margarine
3 heaping tablespoons cocoa
1/4 cup milk

1 pound powdered sugar
1 tablespoon vanilla
1 cup pecans, chopped

Prepare cake: mix sugar and flour in a large bowl. In a saucepan, combine margarine, cocoa, water and shortening; bring to a boil and pour over flour and sugar mixture. Stir and mix well. Add buttermilk, eggs, soda and vanilla. Pour in a jelly roll pan and bake at 400 degrees for 20 minutes. During last 5 to 10 minutes of baking, prepare frosting.
Frosting: in a saucepan, combine margarine, cocoa and milk. Cook over low heat until mixture is hot. Pour hot mixture over powdered sugar and vanilla. Mix until smooth. Add nuts. Stir, then pour over hot cake. This mixture will be thick but it will spread over hot cake. NOTE: if frosting seems too thick add 1 teaspoon milk, one teaspoon at a time, until desired consistency is achieved. Thick frosting spreads easier when cake is frosted while it is hot.

"This cake is a favorite whenever it is served (not just in Texas). Preparation and clean up time is less than 1 hour - start to finish."
Betty Bundy   **Hidden Valley Middle School, Escondido, CA**

APPLE LASAGNA

Serves 12 - 15   **AMERICANA**

2 cups cheddar cheese, shredded
1 cup ricotta cheese
1 egg, lightly beaten
1/4 cup granulated sugar
1 teaspoon almond extract
2 (20 ounce) cans apple pie filling
8 lasagna noodles, cooked, rinsed and drained

6 tablespoons all-purpose flour
6 tablespoons brown sugar, firmly packed,
1/4 cup quick-cooking oats
1/2 teaspoon ground cinnamon
dash ground nutmeg
3 tablespoons margarine

Garnish:
1 cup sour cream
1/3 cup brown sugar, firmly packed

Combine cheddar cheese, ricotta cheese, egg, sugar and almond extract in a medium bowl; blend well. Spread 1 can apple pie filling over bottom of a greased 13" x 9" pan. Layer 1/2 of the noodles over filling, then spread cheese mixture over noodles. Top with remaining noodles, then remaining can of apple pie filling. Combine flour, 6 tablespoons brown sugar, oats, cinnamon and nutmeg in a small bowl. Cut in margarine until crumbly. Sprinkle over apple pie filling. Bake in a preheated 350 degree oven for 45 minutes. Cool 15 minutes. Meanwhile, prepare garnish by blending sour cream and 1/3 cup brown sugar in a small bowl until smooth. Cover; refrigerate. To serve, cut lasagna into squares and garnish with sour cream mixture.

"We found this recipe in the Collector's Edition 'Great American Favorite Brand Name Cookbook'. The students tried it out, and it was really good. I wasn't sure about it when they showed me the recipe, but needless to say - it was a surprise!"

Darlene Haws   **Highland High School, Bakersfield, CA**

ASIA

Burma
China
Hong Kong
Indonesia
Japan
Korea
Thailand

It is recorded that Confucius, twenty-five centuries ago, lectured against eating "anything over-cooked, under-cooked, untidily cut or deficient in seasoning." Such is the basis for the distinct personality of Chinese cuisine. The task of cutting food is confined to the kitchen, thus eliminating the need for such savage implements as knives and making chopsticks the perfect utensil.

The Chinese hold a special respect for the art of cooking. This attitude has developed over the centuries of finding the most economical and nutritious ways of feeding the largest population in the world. They were the first people to control the use of fire and to practice crop rotation. A scarcity of fuel led to the fascinating method of stir-frying, which also preserved flavor and nutritional benefits.

Japanese foods have been greatly influenced by the Chinese. However, it has many unique aspects such as decorative simplicity and freshness of raw materials. The greatest treat a Japanese host can offer his guests is the "first of the season" of any foods.

"The Land of Morning Calm," or Korea, as we know it, has both Chinese and Japanese aspects to its food. Koreans are known as hearty eaters. Their thick soups, called kooks, are served with Chinese-type rice and kimchee pickles.

Asia

SWEET AND SOUR SAUCE (FOR WON TONS & EGG ROLLS)

Makes 3 cups   **CHINA**

1 1/2 cups catsup
2/3 cup brown sugar
2/3 cup granulated sugar

1/2 teaspoon cinnamon
2 slices fresh ginger root
1 lemon, juice only

Mix all of the ingredients in a medium saucepan and bring to a boil over low heat. Cook for 45 minutes, over low heat, stirring occasionally. Remove ginger root before serving.

"We have a won ton and egg roll lab, and one of my students offered this recipe to use. We all loved the sauce and have been using it ever since."

Carole Jackson   **Apple Valley High School, Apple Valley, CA**

WON TONS

Makes about 3 dozen   **CHINA**

1 pound ground turkey
1 (4 1/2 ounce) can small shrimp,
*   drained*
1 egg
1/2 cup onion, diced

1/4 cup Chinese water chestnuts,
*   finely chopped*
1/4 teaspoon salt
1/4 teaspoon pepper
1 package won ton skins

Brown ground turkey in a small saucepan. Drain off grease. Place browned turkey in bowl and add shrimp, egg, onion, water chestnuts, salt and pepper; mix together. Place a small amount of filling in center of won ton skin and roll opposite ends together, then roll and seal edges with a small amount of water. Place on a cookie sheet. Heat oil in deep fryer to 375 degrees. Deep fry won tons, a few at a time, until they become golden brown, drain on paper towels.

Jill Sweet-Gregory   **Santa Paula High School, Santa Paula, CA**

CRAB RANGOON WON TONS

Makes about 3 dozen   **BURMA**

1/2 pound crab OR 1 (8 ounce) can crab
1 (8 ounce) package cream cheese,
*   softened*
2 green onions, chopped
1/2 teaspoon prepared horseradish
1/2 teaspoon fresh lemon juice

1/8 teaspoon hot pepper sauce
dash of pepper
dash of salt
1 package won ton wrappers
2 to 4 cups peanut or corn oil

Combine all ingredients except won ton wrappers and oil; mix well. Place 1 teaspoonful of filling in center of won ton skin. Moisten edges of won ton; fold diagonally and seal edges. Place on waxed paper covered with a thin layer of cornstarch. Cover with plastic wrap; repeat until all filling is used. Keep covered and refrigerate at least 1 hour or overnight. In a wok or heavy fry pan, heat 2 inches of oil to 350 degrees. Cook crab rangoon wontons, without crowding, turning occasionally until crisp and golden brown, about 2 to 3 minutes. Drain on paper towels.

NOTE: If made in advance, keep warm in a 250 degree oven for up to 1 hour.

June Muraoka   Cypress High School, Cypress, CA

CHINESE MEATBALLS

Serves 10 - 12   CHINA

Meatballs:

1 (20 ounce) can water chestnuts, sliced	*3 eggs*
1 bunch green onions, sliced	*1 1/2 teaspoons salt*
2 1/2 pounds ground pork	*1 1/4 cups bread crumbs*
2 tablespoons soy sauce	

Sauce:

1 cup vinegar	*2 tablespoons soy sauce*
2 cups pineapple juice	*3 tablespoons fresh ginger*
3/4 cup sugar	*1/2 cup cornstarch*
2 cups consomme	*1 cup cold water*

Mix together meatball ingredients and roll into balls. Roll in cornstarch and pan fry in oil until cooked, about 30 minutes. Mix sauce together in a saucepan. Combine 1/2 cup cornstarch and 1 cup cold water and add to sauce. Cook until clear and thickened. Serve meatballs in sauce.

Carol O'Keefe   Canyon, Anaheim, CA

CHA SHU (PORK STRIPS)

Serves 6   CHINA

2 pounds pork loin, boned	*3 tablespoons sugar, divided*
1 piece ginger, crushed	*1 tablespoon sake*
3/4 cup water	*dash of pepper*
3 tablespoons soy sauce, divided	*red food coloring*

Cut pork into 5 or 6 long strips. heat ginger, water, 2 tablespoons soy sauce, 2 tablespoons sugar, sake, pepper and food coloring to the boiling point. Add meat and boil 20 to 25 minutes with pan covered, using medium flame. Remove meat. There will be about 1 cup of liquid. To the liquid, add 1 tablespoon sugar and 1 tablespoon soy sauce. Boil this down to 1/2 cup. Sauce will be syrupy. Dip meat in and dry under broiler. Dip meat again in syrup and cool. Slice thin and serve warm or cold.

"This is a delicious appetizer and can be put on top of noodles."

Carol Drescher   Camarillo High School, Camarillo, CA

STAR ANISE CHICKEN WINGS

Serves 4   **CHINA**

16 chicken wings
1/4 cup brown sugar, firmly packed
1/2 cup sherry wine
1/2 cup soy sauce

2 tablespoons sesame oil
4 - 5 whole star anise pods (Chinese spice)
2 green onions, chopped

Cut each chicken wing at the joint, discarding wing tip; place in deep pan. Add brown sugar, sherry, soy sauce, oil and star anise pods. Mix to coat chicken and bring to a boil, then cook over low to medium heat for 1/2 hour, covered, stirring occasionally. Remove lid and cook another 20 - 30 minutes, gently stirring occasionally. When liquid has become a thick syrup, coating the chicken, remove from heat. Be sure to take out all the anise star pods before serving. Allow chicken wings to cool so they may be eaten as a finger food.

"Wonderful party food. I serve these for football parties."

Patti Bartholomew   Casa Roble Fundamental H.S., Orangevale, CA

ORIENTAL FRIED CHICKEN

Serves 8 - 10   **JAPAN**

3 1/2 pounds chicken wings
1/4 cup flour
1/2 cup cornstarch
1/4 cup sugar
1 tablespoon salt

5 tablespoons soy sauce
2 eggs
2 tablespoons green onions, chopped
1 teaspoons fresh ginger, grated
oil for deep frying

Cut off the tips of the chicken wings, then cut the wings apart, set aside. Combine all other ingredients in a large bowl, mix well. Add chicken wings and marinate for at least 2 hours. (May be marinated overnight.) Stir every so often. Heat oil in a large pan or wok. Deep fry chicken wings about 8 to 10 minutes, until outside is golden brown and inside is cooked."

"A different fried chicken. Great for picnics!"

Reiko Ikkanda   South Pasadena Middle School, South Pasadena, CA

ARARE (PARTY MIX)

Serves 8 - 10   **JAPAN**

1/2 cup butter
1/2 cup sugar
1/2 cup light Karo syrup

2 tablespoons soy sauce
10 - 12 dashes tabasco sauce
1 large box Crispix cereal

Optional items:
gold fish crackers
pretzels
nuts

crisp Chinese noodles
popcorn
any ready-mix snack tidbits

Bring first five ingredients to a rolling boil in a large saucepan. Place cereal mix in a large foil-lined roasting pan. Pour syrup over mixture. Toss to coat. Bake at 250 degrees for 1 hour, stirring every 15 minutes. Spread out on newspaper that has been covered with paper towels to cool. Store in airtight container.

NOTE: VERY optional: during last 15 minutes of baking, you can add 1/2 cup Furikake Shirakiku (California-type seaweed and horseradish powder).

"My cousin, Liz, gave me this recipe. Everyone makes it to their liking, depending on the optional items they choose."

Sharon F. Yonehara   **Big Valley High School, Beiber, CA**

THAI RICE CHIPS

Serves 6   THAILAND

1/2 cup water   *1 teaspoon salt*
1 cup dried shrimp*   *2 teaspoons pepper*
3 cups rice flour

*Purchase at Thai food store

Blend the ingredients in a large bowl forming dough. Roll the dough into a 1" diameter log about 6" long. Steam the log for about 3 minutes. Let the log dry. Using a sharp knife, cut lengthwise into strips; cut the strips into 1" chips. Dry the chips in the sun, dehydrating machine, or a warm oven. Fry the chips in hot vegetable oil (if oil smokes, it is too hot). Cook until they begin to look puffed (about 1 minute). Serve immediately. Uncooked chips will keep in a tightly sealed container in the refrigerator about 1 month.

"These chips are delicious. They are commonly made in Thailand. I got this recipe from a student whose mother is from Thailand."

Judy Henry   **Mission Viejo High School, Mission Viejo, CA**

SUAPI AMI KURI ALA KATIE

Serves many   JAPAN

4 large cucumbers   *1/2 cup vinegar*
1/2 cup sugar   *1/4 cup shoyu*soy sauce*

Peel cucumbers, discard ends and slice as thinly as possibly, crosswise. Do not discard seeds. Place cucumbers in a bowl and pour sugar, vinegar and shoyu over them; mix gently until sugar is dissolved. Let sit in refrigerator 30 minutes or more. Stir before serving. May be kept refrigerated up to 3 days.

NOTE: Japanese feel that the bitterness which is sometimes in cucumbers can be extracted by cutting 1/2" off the darker green end and briskly rubbing the cut ends together until a froth forms.

*Shoyu is a very mild soy sauce. If using Chinese or American soy sauce, decrease amount to 3 tablespoons.

"My daughter made these for her 7th grade class during a unit on Japan and everyone enjoyed them."

Brenda Burke   **Mt. Whitney High School, Visalia, CA**

Hot and Sour Soup, Page 31

Pork and Broccoli Stir-Fry, Page 43

Spicy Indonesian Noodles, Page 40

Classic Chicken Chow Mein, Page 39

CHINESE CHICKEN SALAD

Serves 1   CHINA

Dressing:
1/2 teaspoon dry mustard
3 tablespoons sugar
1 tablespoon soy sauce
1/4 cup salad oil

3 tablespoons rice vinegar
1/4 teaspoon black pepper
1/4 teaspoon salt

1 chicken breast, cooked and shredded
1/2 package slivered almonds, toasted
oil for frying

1/4 package rice sticks, fried
1/4 head lettuce, shredded

Wrap chicken in foil and bake at 400 degrees for 1 hour. Cool and shred meat. Spread almonds out on baking sheet and bake in oven until brown. Heat oil over medium heat. Fry rice sticks quickly and remove from oil with tongs before they begin to brown. (Rice sticks cook and puff up within seconds of being added to hot oil.) Drain on paper towels.

Combine chicken, lettuce and almonds and toss with dressing. Top with rice sticks and toss gently.

"It's a family favorite."

Myra Skidmore   **Downey High School, Downey, CA**

CHINOIS CHICKEN SALAD

Serves 4   CHINA

4 cups cooked chicken, cut julienne style
6 cups Napa cabbage, shredded
1 cup green cabbage, shredded
1 cup red cabbage, shredded
2 cups mixed salad greens, torn

1 cup carrots, shredded
6 green onions, sliced
1 cup jicama, cut julienne style
4 - 6 cups crisp fried wonton strips

Dressing:
2 tablespoons dry Chinese hot mustard
1/2 teaspoon garlic powder
1 teaspoon ground pepper
2 tablespoons honey

1/2 cup seasoned rice vinegar
1 tablespoon sesame oil
1/2 cup vegetable oil

Roast a chicken or use leftovers. In a large bowl, combine cabbages, salad greens, carrots, green onions and jicama. Add 3 1/2 cups chicken, 1/2 of the wonton strips. Mix all ingredients for dressing and whisk thoroughly; toss well into salad mixture. Serve with remaining chicken arranged on top and sprinkle with remaining wonton strips.

"Flour tortilla strips will work well in place of wonton strips."

Val Herford   **Mesa Intermediate School, Palmdale, CA**

CHINESE NOODLE SLAW

Serves 10

1 medium head cabbage, chopped
5 green onions, chopped (include some
   green tops)
1/4 cup margarine

2 (3 ounce) packages Ramen noodles
1 tablespoon sesame seeds
1/2 cup almonds, slivered

Dressing:
1/2 cup vegetable oil
1 tablespoon soy sauce

1/3 cup sugar
1/4 cup vinegar

In a large bowl, combine cabbage and onions. Chill. Break noodles into small pieces. In a saucepan, melt margarine over medium-low heat; brown noodles, sesame seeds and almonds, stirring frequently. Drain on paper towels. Combine all dressing ingredients in a mixing bowl; blend with a wire whisk. Twenty minutes before serving, toss noodle mixture with cabbage and onions. Pour dressing over slaw and mix well.

"This recipe came from a friend - Ginger Kemp."

Glenell Fuller   **Glendora High School, Glendora, CA**

ORIENTAL SPINACH SALAD

Serves 4 - 6   CHINA

1 quart spinach, washed and cut
1 cup mandarin oranges, drained
2 tablespoons vegetable oil
2 tablespoons rice wine vinegar

2 tablespoons apple juice
4 teaspoons sesame seeds
slivered almonds, optional

Toss washed and cut spinach with drained mandarin oranges in salad bowl. In another small bowl, mix oil, vinegar and apple juice. Pour over salad. Sprinkle with sesame seeds and slivered almonds, if desired.

"This colorful salad is an easy and delicious way to serve spinach."

Renee Browning   **Hesperia High School, Hesperia, CA**

PEKING SPINACH SALAD

Serves 8   CHINA

12 won ton skins (3 inch squares)
1 1/2 quarts (3/4 pound) spinach leaves,
   rinsed and crisped
1/4 pound mushrooms, rinsed and sliced
   thin

3/4 cup carrots, sliced
2 medium-firm plums, red skinned,
   sliced thin

Plum dressing:
1/3 cup plum jam
1 tablespoon soy sauce

3 tablespoons lemon juice
1/2 teaspoon ground cinnamon

Quarter won ton skins and lay them flat on greased 12" x 15" baking sheet; spray or brush with water. Bake at 500 degrees for 3 minutes, watching carefully.

Whisk together dressing ingredients in a small bowl. Place spinach in a large bowl and arrange won tons, mushrooms, carrots and plums on top. Gently toss with Plum Dressing. Serve immediately.

Sue Waterbury   San Luis Obispo High School, San Luis Obispo, CA

ORIENTAL-STYLE HOT AND SOUR SOUP

Serves 6   CHINA

*1 3/4 pounds boneless beef chuck arm
  pot roast
1/4 cup reduced sodium soy sauce
5 cups water, divided
1 tablespoon instant beef bouillon
  granules
4 ounces fresh mushrooms, sliced*
1 (8 ounce) can bamboo shots, sliced,
  drained and cut into thin strips
3 tablespoons red wine vinegar*

*1/4 teaspoon crushed red pepper
2 tablespoons cornstarch
1 egg, well beaten
4 ounces firm tofu, cut into thin strips
2 teaspoons Oriental dark-roasted
  sesame oil
2 green onions, thinly sliced
  diagonally*

Trim excess fat from pot roast; cut across the grain into 2" x 1/8" x 1/8" strips. Pour soy sauce over beef strips, stirring to coat. Combine 4 1/2 cups water and bouillon granules in Dutch oven; bring to a boil. Add beef mixture. Reduce heat; cover tightly and simmer 1 hour or until beef is tender. Stir in mushrooms, bamboo shoots, wine vinegar and pepper pods. Simmer, uncovered, 10 minutes. Dissolve cornstarch in remaining 1/2 cup water; gradually stir into soup and continue cooking until slightly thickened. Slowly pour egg, in a thin stream, into soup, stirring constantly to form fine shreds. Add tofu; cook until heated through. Remove from heat. Stir in sesame oil. Garnish with green onions.

*One half of 1 ounce package dried shiitake mushrooms may be substituted for fresh mushrooms. To prepare shiitake mushrooms, soak in warm water to cover approximately 30 minutes. Remove and discard stems; slice tops into strips.

National Live Stock and Meat Board   Chicago, IL

SHIITAKE MUSHROOM SOUP

Serves 4   JAPAN

*1 yellow onion
1 clove garlic, chopped fine
2 tablespoons peanut oil
2 dashes sesame oil
1 dash chili oil
1/4 pound Shiitake mushrooms
1 small head bok choy (or other Chinese
  greens), chopped*

*1/4 cup dry Reisling
1 tablespoon fresh ginger, chopped
5 cups good (homemade if possible)
  beef broth
2 tablespoons soy sauce*

Saute onion and garlic in oils until soft. Add mushrooms and bok choy and saute until just wilted. Add wine, ginger, boiling beef broth and soy sauce. Cook for 5 minutes. Serve.

Sally Paul   Winters High School, Winters, CA

CHINESE BROCCOLI

Serves 6   CHINA

2 pounds broccoli, trimmed of stalks   *1 (5 ounce) can water chestnuts, diced*
1/2 cup butter   *2 tablespoons onion, minced*
1 teaspoon salt   *1/4 cup lemon juice*
pepper to taste   *2 tablespoons soy sauce*

Cut broccoli into serving pieces. Cook in a small amount of water until tender; drain. Melt butter; add salt and pepper, water chestnuts and onion. Cook over medium heat 2 to 3 minutes. Add lemon juice and soy sauce. Toss broccoli with sauce and heat thoroughly.

Marjorie Brown   **Cabrillo High School, Lompoc, CA**

CHINESE BAKED PEAS

Serves 6   CHINA

1/2 cup onion, thinly sliced   *1 (10 1/2 ounce) can cream of*
1 large can mushrooms, sliced and   *mushroom soup*
*   drained*   *1/3 cup milk*
1/4 cup butter   *1 teaspoon salt*
1 (10 ounce) package frozen green peas, *dash of pepper*
*   slightly thawed, broken apart*   *1 cup chow mein noodles*
1 (1 pound) can bean sprouts, drained
1 (8 ounce) can water chestnuts,
*   sliced and drained*

Saute onions and mushrooms with butter until soft. Add peas, bean sprouts and water chestnuts. In a separate bowl, blend soup, milk, salt and pepper. Pour over vegetable mixture and mix carefully. Place in a 1 1/2 quart shallow casserole. Edge casserole with chow mein noodles. Bake at 350 degrees for 30 - 40 minutes.

"Delicious compliment with any meat, but particularly good with beef."

Marilyn Bankhead   **San Marcos High School, San Marcos, CA**

FRIED RICE

Serves 4   CHINA

1 cup rice, cooked and cooled   *1/2 package of fried rice mix*
4 strips bacon, cooked and diced   *1 green onion, sliced thin*
1 - 2 tablespoons soy sauce   *2 eggs, well beaten*

After frying bacon, remove bacon from pan. Stir in cold rice and heat on medium-high heat. Sprinkle with soy sauce. Stir in fried rice mix, green onion and bacon. Stir carefully. Push rice mixture to one side of pan. Pour egg mixture in remaining part of pan and cook by stirring until done. Break scrambled eggs into size of small peas. Mix all ingredients in the pan together and serve well heated. NOTE: More soy sauce may be used if desired.

"Students love preparing this recipe!"

Betty Byrne   **Vaca Pena Middle School, Vacaville, CA**

TERIYAKI SAUCE FOR BEEF AND CHICKEN

Makes 2 cups   **JAPAN**

1 cup sugar
1 cup soy sauce
1 square inch fresh ginger root
3 - 4 cloves garlic, crushed
London broil (1/4 to 1/2 pound per person)

Chicken, boneless and skinless and/or
London broil (1/4-1/2 lb. per
person)

Peel or scrape skin from ginger root. Grate (easiest when frozen). Combine all ingredients except meat. Use as a marinade for London broil (have butcher thinly slice diagonally). Marinate beef 2 hours or more depending upon size and amount. BBQ or broil until pink disappears. If using with chicken, BBQ or coat with flour and fry, then dip in teriyaki sauce for flavor.

"This recipe comes from the best P.E. teacher I ever had, Luirlene Fujii. We now work together at Rancho Starbuck where all the teachers demand her beef and chicken teriyaki luncheon at least once every year."

Chris Henry   Rancho Starbuck Junior High School, Whittier, CA

KOREAN RIBS

Serves 6   **KOREA**

3 pounds flank steak or butterflied short
*   ribs*
4 teaspoons sesame seeds, pulverized
4 tablespoons sugar
1/2 teaspoon black pepper

2 - 3 green onions, chopped
1/2 to 3/4 cup soy sauce
1/2 cup sesame oil
dash Accent (optional)
2 cloves garlic, minced

Score meat; mix remaining ingredients together. Pour marinade over meat and marinate at least 4 hours or overnight. Broil or barbeque.

"This is my favorite marinade."

Maria Hoffman   Katella High School, Anaheim, CA

WON TON & FLANK STEAK

Serves 6   **JAPAN**

1 pound ground pork
1/4 cup + 2 tablespoons cornstarch,
*   divided*
4 teaspoons garlic powder, divided
1 package won ton skins

2 pounds flank steak, frozen
2 tablespoons oil
1 cup water
1/4 cup soy sauce

Combine pork, 2 tablespoons cornstarch and 2 teaspoons garlic powder. Place a small amount of mixture onto a won ton skin, folding opposite corners over meat mixture, then fold one of the remaining corners up to meet other 2 sides. Seal with water (a corner will be left up for easy handling). Set aside. Thinly slice frozen flank steak. Cook quickly in oil; add water, soy sauce, 2 teaspoons garlic powder and 1/4 cup cornstarch. Cook until thick. While you are preparing steak, bring a large pot of water to a boil. Drop won tons into boiling water and cook until won tons rise to the surface. To serve: place cooked won tons on plate; top with steak.

Linda Silvasy   **Olive Peirce Middle School, Ramona, CA**

KOREAN FLANK STEAK

Serves 6 - 8   **KOREA**

3 - 4 pounds flank steak (ask butcher to
    "tenderize")
bottled Teriyaki Marinade sauce
2 - 3 eggs, lightly beaten

3 - 4 green onions, chopped
flour, for coating
1 cup bread crumbs
oil, for frying

Marinate steak in teriyaki marinade at least 1 hour, preferably overnight. Cut steak into 3 to 4 equal strips, cutting across the width of the steak. Combine eggs and green onions. Dip each section of steak in flour, then egg/onion mixture, then in bread crumbs. Refrigerate steaks for 30 minutes. Heat oil very hot, then add steaks and immediately lower heat to low, cooking slowly for 25 to 30 minutes. Drain on paper towels. Let set 15 to 20 minutes. Slice steaks into small 1/2 inch pieces. Serve.

"This is a favorite of everyone who has ever tried it. It's definitely worth the work. Tastes great hot or cold."

Libby Newman   **West Valley High School, Hemet, CA**

ORIENTAL PEPPER STEAK

Serves 4   **CHINA**

1 pound round steak, cut into small pieces
2 tablespoons oil
1 tablespoon flour
1/2 cup catsup
1/2 cup water
3 tablespoons soy sauce
1/4 teaspoon pepper

1 cube beef bouillon
1 clove garlic, minced
1/2 cup onion, chopped
8 ounces mushrooms, sliced
2 large bell peppers, sliced
2 medium onions, sliced

Brown meat in oil; remove. Blend flour in remaining oil. Add catsup, water, soy sauce, pepper, bouillon cube, garlic and chopped onion. Bring to a boil; lower heat to simmer for 10 minutes. Return meat to sauce and simmer for 30 minutes, or until tender. Ten minutes before serving, add mushrooms, bell peppers and sliced onions. Cook until tender, about ten minutes. Serve on fluffy rice.

Carol Kagy   **Norwalk High School, Norwalk, CA**

BROCCOLI BEEF

Serves 4 - 5   CHINA

1 pound flank steak, cut into
   1/8" x 1 1/2" slices
1 tablespoon & 2 teaspoons cornstarch,
   divided
1 teaspoon sugar
2 tablespoons light soy sauce
3 - 4 tablespoons water
3 - 4 tablespoons peanut oil for stir frying

1 pound fresh broccoli, cut into
   flowerettes
1 clove garlic, minced
1 slice ginger root, minced
1/2 cup chicken stock
2 tablespoons oyster sauce

Marinate beef in 1 tablespoon cornstarch, sugar, soy sauce and 1 tablespoon water for 1 hour. Heat a wok or skillet. Add 2 tablespoons peanut oil and stir fry broccoli for about 1 minute. Add 2 to 3 tablespoons water and cover to steam the broccoli until just barely tender (3-4 minutes). Lower heat slightly and stir frequently to prevent scorching. Remove broccoli and set aside. Heat wok again and add 2 tablespoons peanut oil, garlic and ginger root. Stir. Add flank steak, a little at a time, stir frying until the meat is browned on the outside and pink in the middle. Push the meat up the sides of the wok and add more meat in the center of the wok until all the meat in the center is browned. Stir 2 tablespoons cornstarch, chicken stock and oyster sauce; add gradually to the wok. Stir and scrape the bottom of the wok if necessary until the sauce thickens and bubbles. Place the broccoli in the wok and gently combine all ingredients. Serve immediately with rice.

"This recipe has become a favorite one with our students. The recipe was obtained from Wei-ling Louie, a Chinese cooking instructor."

Bonnie Landin   **Garden Grove High School, Garden Grove, CA**

SZECHWAN BEEF STIR-FRY

Serves 4   CHINA

1 pound beef flank steak
2 tablespoons reduced sodium soy sauce
4 teaspoons dark roasted sesame oil
1 1/2 teaspoons sugar
1 teaspoon cornstarch
2 cloves garlic, crushed
1 tablespoon fresh ginger, minced

1/4 teaspoon crushed red pepper pods
1 small red bell pepper, cut into 1 inch
   pieces
1 (8 ounce) package frozen baby corn,
   defrosted
1/4 pound pea pods, julienned

Cut beef steak lengthwise into 2 strips; slice across the grain into 1/8 inch thick strips. Combine soy sauce, 2 teaspoons oil, sugar and cornstarch. Stir into strips. Heat remaining 2 teaspoons oil in large skillet over medium heat. Add garlic, ginger and red pepper pods; cook 30 seconds. Add bell pepper and corn; stir-fry 1 1/2 minutes. Add pea pods; stir-fry another 30 seconds. Remove vegetables from the skillet and reserve. Stir-fry beef strips (half at a time) 2 to 3 minutes. Return vegetables and beef to skillet and heat through.

"Serve this with white rice. You may use a wok or a frying pan instead of a skillet."

Phyllis Arkus   **Lakewood High School, Lakewood, CA**

CASHEW CHICKEN

Serves 4 - 6   **CHINA**

3/4 pound chicken breast, boneless
*   and skinless*
1 1/2 tablespoons cornstarch
2 tablespoons dry sherry or sake
1 1/2 tablespoons soy sauce
5 tablespoons oil, divided

1 1/2 green peppers, cut in 1/2 inch
*   squares*
6 water chestnuts, diced
1/4 pound fresh mushrooms, diced
2 - 3 tablespoons hoisin sauce
1/4 cup cashews, roasted

Cut chicken into 1/2" squares. Marinate chicken in cornstarch, sherry and soy sauce. Heat 2 tablespoons oil in wok. Add green peppers, water chestnuts and mushrooms. Stir fry over medium heat for 2 - 3 minutes. Remove from wok and set aside. Heat 3 tablespoons oil in wok over high heat. Add chicken and stir-fry for 2 - 3 minutes until chicken turns white. Add hoisin sauce; stir. Add cooked vegetables and cook 2 minutes more. Stir in cashews and heat 1 to 2 minutes. Serve with rice and enjoy!

Sue Hope   **Lompoc High School, Lompoc, CA**

SZECHWAN CHICKEN WITH CASHEWS (GAI DING)

Serves 6   **CHINA**

2 whole chicken breasts
1 egg white
1 tablespoon +1 teaspoon cornstarch,
*   divided*
1 1/2 teaspoons salt
1 teaspoons ginger root, finely chopped
1 tablespoon +1 teaspoon soy sauce,
*   divided*
dash pepper
4 tablespoons vegetable oil, divided

1 cup raw cashews
6 green onions, chopped
1 large green pepper, cut into
*   1/2 inch squares*
1 (14 ounce) can button mushrooms,
*   drained (reserve liquid)*
1 teaspoon dried red pepper, chopped
1/2 cup chicken broth
1 tablespoon water

Remove bones and skin from chicken breasts; cut into 1/2 inch pieces. Mix egg white, 1 teaspoon cornstarch, 1 teaspoon salt, ginger root, 1 teaspoon soy sauce and dash of pepper in a 2 quart glass bowl, stir in chicken. Cover and refrigerate at least 30 minutes. Heat 1 tablespoon oil in wok or 10 inch skillet until hot. Stir-fry cashews until light brown, about 1 minute; drain on paper towels. Sprinkle with 1/2 teaspoon salt. Heat 2 tablespoons oil until hot. Add chicken; stir-fry until chicken turns white, about 3 minutes. Remove chicken. Heat remaining 1 tablespoon oil until hot. Add green onions, green pepper, mushrooms and dried red pepper. Stir-fry about 1 minute. Add chicken, chicken broth and reserved mushroom liquid; heat to boiling. Mix remaining 1 tablespoon cornstarch with water and 1 tablespoon soy sauce; stir into chicken mixture. Cook and stir until thickened, about 1 minute. Stir in cashews; garnish with green onion tops.

"Serve with steamed or boiled rice."

Deborah Weiss   **Ayala High School, Chino, CA**

CHINESE WALNUT CHICKEN

Serves 4   CHINA

1 cup walnuts	2 tablespoons sherry
1/4 cup oil	1 1/4 cups chicken broth
3 chicken breasts, cut into cubes	1 cup onion, sliced
1/2 teaspoon salt	1 1/2 cups celery
1 tablespoon cornstarch	bamboo shots
1 teaspoon sugar	water chestnuts
1/4 cup soy sauce	

In skillet or wok, toast walnuts in oil; remove. Cook chicken with salt in oil for 5 - 10 minutes. Combine cornstarch, sugar, soy sauce, sherry and 3/4 cup broth; set aside. Add onion, celery and 1/2 cup broth to chicken; cook 5 minutes. Add vegetables and soy sauce mixture. Cook until thick. Serve with rice.

Debbie L. Rothe   **Alta Loma High School, Alta Loma, CA**

SESAME GINGER CHICKEN

Serves 4   CHINA

1 tablespoon sesame seeds, toasted	vegetable cooking spray
2 teaspoons ginger, grated .	green onion, cut into thin strips for
2 tablespoons honey	garnish (optional)
2 tablespoons reduced sodium soy sauce	
4 (4 ounce) chicken breasts, skinned and boned	

Combine first 4 ingredients in a small bowl, stir well and set aside. Place chicken between 2 sheets of heavy duty plastic wrap and flatten to 1/4 inch thickness, using a meat mallet or rolling pin. Coat grill rack with cooking spray; place grill over medium-hot coals. Place chicken on rack and cook 4 minutes on each side, basting frequently with soy sauce mixture. Transfer chicken to a serving platter; garnish with green onion, if desired.

"This is quick, easy and healthy. We eat a lot of chicken in our household and this recipes gives chicken an oriental flavor. We love it!"

Sue Zallar   **Capistrano Valley High School, San Juan Capistrano, CA**

WEST COAST ORIENTAL CHICKEN

Serves 4 - 6   CHINA

1 pound chicken breasts, boneless , cut into strips	1 (6 ounce) can mushrooms, drained
2 tablespoons margarine	1 (8 ounce) can water chestnuts, drained
1 cup celery, chopped	1 (4 ounce) jar pimento
1 bunch green onions, chopped	1 can golden mushroom soup
2 tablespoons soy sauce	

In a 10 inch skillet, brown chicken strips in margarine. Add all remaining ingredients and simmer for 15 to 20 minutes, stirring occasionally. Serve over rice. Top with crisp noodles, if desired.

"This simple recipe is always a winner!"

Linda Woolley   **La Sierra High School, Riverside, CA**

CHICKEN CHOP SUEY

Serves 4 - 6   **CHINA**

fresh ginger root
1 teaspoon salt
4 - 6 chicken breasts, cut into bite sized
    pieces
oil for stir frying
1/2 cup carrots, sliced diagonally
1/2 cup celery, sliced diagonally
1/2 cup onions, thinly sliced
1/2 cup carrots, sliced diagonally

1/2 cup fresh broccoli flowerets, cut
    into small pieces
1 tablespoon sherry (optional)
2 teaspoons sugar
1/2 cup roasted peanuts (optional)
3/4 cup chicken stock
1 tablespoon cornstarch
1 tablespoon water

Rub sides of wok with fresh ginger. Add salt to chicken and stir fry in approximately 2 to 3 tablespoons oil in wok. Stir fry for 2 to 3 minutes until all pink color is gone from chicken. Drain chicken and remove from wok. Add 2 tablespoons of oil to wok and stir fry carrots, celery, onions and broccoli for 2 to 3 minutes, or until slightly tender. Add chicken to vegetables. Add soy sauce, sherry, sugar and dry roasted peanuts. Stir, adding chicken stock for 2 minutes. Dissolve cornstarch in water and add to chicken and vegetables. Cook 1 minute until thickened. Serve over rice.

Leslie Rodden   **San Gorgonia High School, San Bernardino, CA**

CHICKEN STIR-FRY WITH ZUCCHNI

Serves 4   **CHINA**

1 cup chicken breast, diced
1 clove garlic, crushed
oil for frying
2 tablespoons light soy sauce
1/4 cup canned mushrooms, sliced
1 1/2 cups zucchini, sliced

1/2 cup bamboo shoots, sliced into
    matchsticks
1 tablespoon cornstarch
1/4 cup water
almonds, roasted and slivered

Stir fry chicken over high heat with garlic in oil. When it turns white, add soy sauce and continue stirring for several minutes. Add zucchini, mushrooms and bamboo shoots; cover and cook a few minutes. Dissolve cornstarch in water and add to mixture; stir for about 1 minute. Garnish with roasted slivered almonds and serve over rice.

"This is a great recipe to use at home and in the foods classroom."

Wanda Shelton   **Newport Harbor High School, Newport Beach, CA**

BAHMI

Serves 4 - 6 INDONESIA

1/2 pound Chinese vermicelli
3/4 cup vegetable oil
4 chicken breasts, boiled
1 1/2 cup green onion, thinly sliced
2 cloves garlic, minced

4 cups cabbage, shredded
1/2 cup soy sauce
1/2 teaspoon black pepper
2 eggs, beaten

Following directions on noodle package, boil until tender; drain. Heat 2 tablespoons oil in skillet and saute chicken 3 minutes. Remove and add 2 more tablespoons oil; saute onions and garlic. Remove and add 2 more tablespoons oil; saute cabbage for 3 minutes. Return all sauteed ingredients to pan and add soy sauce and pepper. Cook 2 minutes. In a separate non-stick skillet, heat 2 tablespoons oil until warm; cook beaten eggs until set; cut up and set aside.. Heap noodles onto a platter and put chicken and cabbage mixture on top. Top with cooked egg and serve.

"This is a dish my kids always ask for!"

Sheryl Malone   **Mt. Carmel High School, San Diego, CA**

CLASSIC CHICKEN CHOW MEIN

Serves 4 CHINA

1 pound chicken breasts, boneless,
    skinless, cut into 1/4" x 1 1/2" pieces
1 pound Chinese egg noodles, uncooked
5 tablespoons cooking oil, divided
1/2 teaspoon salt
1 teaspoon sherry
2 cups fresh mushrooms, sliced
1 cup bamboo shoots
1 cup Chinese cabbage, cut diagonally

1 cup water chestnuts, sliced
1 medium onion, cut in wedges,
    then halved
2 ribs celery, cut diagonally
1 green pepper, cut in wedges
1 cup fresh bean sprouts
4 tablespoons cornstarch
1 teaspoon ginger

4 tablespoons soy sauce
1/2 teaspoon MSG (optional)
1/8 teaspoon pepper

1 teaspoon sesame oil
1 teaspoon oyster sauce
1 cup chicken broth, warmed

In large saucepan containing 2 quarts boiling salted water, place noodles and cook about 8 minutes; drain thoroughly. Place 2 tablespoons oil in large wok (or non-stick fry pan) and heat to medium-high temperature. Spread half of the cooked noodles in wok and cook without stirring until light brown, about 3 minutes. Turn the pancake-like noodles and cook the other side until light brown, about 3 minutes; remove to warm platter. Add 1 tablespoon of the oil to wok and repeat with remainder of noodles. In same wok, add remaining 2 tablespoons of the oil and sprinkle with salt. Add chicken and sherry; stir-fry about 3 minutes. Push chicken to side; add mushrooms, bamboo shoots, Chinese cabbage, water chestnuts, onion, celery and green pepper. Stir-fry vegetables about 3 minutes. Add bean sprouts. Mix together chicken and vegetables. In a small bowl, mix together cornstarch and ginger; stir in soy sauce to make a smooth past-like mixture.

- 39 -   **Asia**

Sprinkle chicken and vegetables with MSG (if desired), pepper, sesame oil and oyster sauce. Stir in warm chicken broth and bring to a boil; slowly add cornstarch mixture, stirring to make smooth sauce, about 1 minute. Serve Chow Mein over fried noodles.

National Broiler Council   **Columbia, SC**

GINGERED SCALLOPS

Serves 4   **CHINA**

1 1/2 pounds scallops
flour, for coating
1/4 cup (1/2 stick) butter
2 tablespoons fresh ginger root,
   finely sliced

1 teaspoon salt
freshly ground pepper
2 tablespoons fresh parsley, minced

Sprinkle scallops lightly with flour. Melt butter in large skillet until sizzling. Add scallops with ginger and saute quickly until scallops are lightly browned and cooked through, about 1-2 minutes. Transfer to serving platter, season with salt and pepper and sprinkle with parsley. Serve immediately.

Donna Fippin   **Bret Harte High School, Altaville, CA**

SPICY INDONESIAN NOODLES

Serves 4   **INDONESIA**

8 ounces vermicelli or thin spaghetti,
   uncooked
3 tablespoons peanut or salad oil
1 medium onion, chopped
1 green or red pepper, chopped
2 ribs celery, thinly sliced
1 cup mushrooms, sliced
2 cups cabbage, thinly shredded

3 cloves garlic, crushed
1/4 cup soy sauce
1/2 teaspoon hot red pepper sauce,
   or to taste
8 ounces Surimi seafood, crab
   flavored, chunk or flake style
1 cup mung bean sprouts (optional)

Cook vermicelli according to package directions; rinse in cold water to stop cooking; drain; toss with 1 tablespoon oil; set aside. Add remaining 2 tablespoons oil to heavy 12" skillet over medium heat; stir in onion, green pepper, celery and mushrooms; cook, stirring occasionally, 3 to 5 minutes. Stir in cabbage and garlic, cook and stir another minute, or until cabbage is wilted. Add soy sauce and hot red pepper sauce. Add cooked vermicelli to skillet, lifting with salad fork and spoon tongs to coat with soy sauce and mix with sauteed vegetables. Arrange Surimi seafood over vermicelli; cover; reduce heat to low and cook another 2 to 3 minutes or until seafood is heated through. Serve hot or at room temperature, sprinkled with bean sprouts.

National Fisheries Institute   **Arlington, VA**

NASI GORENG (INDONESIAN FRIED RICE)

Serves 4   INDONESIA

Onion mixture:
2 teaspoons ground red chile peppers
1 onion, minced

3 cloves garlic, minced
dried prawns (optional)

1 1/2 cups rice, cooked and cooled
1 teaspoon salt
2 tablespoons soy sauce
8 strips bacon, cooked and cut into
    small pieces (reserve drippings)
4 eggs, scrambled

2 small cans shrimp
2 small cans olives, sliced
1 small can peas
1/3 cup parsley, chopped
4 scallions, chopped

1 - 2 tomatoes, cut into wedges
1 - 2 lemon wedges

Combine all ingredients for onion mixture; add cooked rice and stir-fry. Add salt and soy sauce. Add bacon, eggs, shrimp, olives and peas and stir-fry until heated through. Top with parsley, scallions and tomatoes. Serve with a lemon wedge.

Peggy Herndon   **Central Valley High School, Central Valley, CA**

KUNG PAO SHRIMP WITH CASHEWS

Serves 4 - 6   CHINA

1 cup raw cashews
1 1/2 tablespoons soy sauce
2 tablespoons red wine vinegar
2 teaspoons sugar
1 teaspoon sesame oil
2 tablespoons peanut oil
1/2 teaspoon salt

8 small dried red chiles
2 teaspoons fresh gingers, minced
2 cloves garlic, minced
1 green or red pepper, cut into
    1 inch squares
1 pound medium shrimp, shelled
    and deveined

Preheat oven to 325 degrees. In flat pan, spread cashews in single layer; roast until golden brown (about 10 minutes), stirring occasionally; set aside. In small bowl, combine soy sauce, vinegar, sugar and sesame oil; set aside. Preheat wok over medium heat until hot, then pour in peanut oil. Add salt and chiles; cook until chiles are charred (about 15 seconds). Add ginger and garlic; stir fry until fragrant and lightly browned. Increase heat to high; add bell pepper and stir-fry until pepper is seared (30 seconds). Add shrimp a handful at a time and stir fry until shrimp are pink and feel firm to touch (about 2 minutes total). Add reserved sauce mixture; toss and stir until sauce thickens to a glaze (about 30 seconds). Remove wok from heat. Gently stir in reserved roasted cashews.

"This is a very elegant dish that is easy to prepare."
Bonnie Shrock   **Kearny High School, San Diego, CA**

STEAMED GINGERED FISH

Serves 4 - 6

CHINA

1 - 2 pound fresh fish
4 green onions, slivered
2 teaspoons salt
1/2 teaspoon MSG (optional)

1/4 cup + 1 tablespoon peanut oil
6 slices ginger root, slivered
1 teaspoon soy salt

Score the fish then place on top of the slivered green onions. Sprinkle the salt and MSG on top of one half of the fish. Pour 1 tablespoon peanut oil over fish. Steam the fish on a plate over boiling water for 6 - 10 minutes. When the fish is transparent, place on a platter and top with ginger, soy sauce and remaining onion. Pour 1/4 cup boiling peanut oil on top and serve immediately.

"This is one of my favorite dishes I enjoyed while living and teaching in Shenzhen, China."

Sandy Ransom   **Tehachapi High School, Tehachapi, CA**

HOT & SPICY TOFU

Serves 4 - 6

CHINA

1 tablespoon cornstarch
2 tablespoons soy sauce
1/4 cup water
3 tablespoons peanut oil, divided
4 cloves garlic, minced
2 green onions, sliced

1 small carrots, sliced
chili peppers to taste
1/2 to 1 pound ground pork or beef
1 1/2 cups tofu, cubed
cooked rice

Mix the cornstarch, soy sauce, water and 1 tablespoon oil in a bowl and set aside. Heat remaining 2 tablespoons oil in a wok or fry pan and stir fry garlic 30 seconds. Add green onions and fry 1 minute. Add carrot and chili peppers and fry 1 minute. Remove ingredients from pan and set aside. Fry ground beef or pork; drain off fat and set aside. Fry tofu cubes for 2 to 3 minutes and then add meat and vegetables and cornstarch mixture. Cook until thick and bubbly. Serve over cooked rice.

"My favorite dish while living in Shenzhen, China. The seasonings make tofu taste good."

Sandy Ransom   **Tehachapi High School, Tehachapi, CA**

QUICK FRIED RICE

Serves 6

CHINA

4 cups long grain rice, cooked and chilled
1 pound sausage, regular or "light"
1 (10 ounce) package frozen mixed
    Oriental-style vegetables, cooked

1/4 cup green onions, minced
1/2 cup mushrooms, chopped
2 eggs, beaten and scrambled

In a large skillet, fry sausage. Add cold rice and stir gently to heat through. Add mixed vegetables, onions and mushroom. Add egg and heat through. Season to with soy sauce.

"My family loves this - we have it often."

Cindy Johnson   **Orland High School, Orland, CA**

CHICKEN FRIED RICE

Serves 4 - 6

3 eggs, beaten
1 tablespoon cooking oil
3 tablespoons green onions, sliced
   (tops included)

Optional:
1/2 cup celery, sliced
1/2 cup water chestnuts, sliced

1/2 cup fresh mushrooms, chopped
4 cups rice, cooked and cooled
3 tablespoons soy sauce
1/2 cup cooked ham, finely diced

1/2 cup Chinese pea pods

Spray a 12" skillet or wok with non-stick cooking spray and then cook beaten eggs in it without stirring, until set. Flip. Invert skillet over a baking sheet or bread board to remove eggs, roll and cut into short, narrow strips. In the same skillet or wok, heat oil and quickly cook onions , mushroom and any other vegetables until tender 3 to 4 minutes. Stir in cooked rice, soy sauce and ham, heat through.

NOTE: sliced celery, water chestnuts, broccoli, Chinese pea pods are other vegetables which may be added.

"This simple economical and nutritious recipe is a favorite among my students. They love to make it AND eat it!"

Phyllis Kaylor   **Ray Kroc Middle School, San Diego, CA**

ANTS CREEPING ON THE TREES

Serves 4 - 6

2 ounces vermicelli (mung bean)
2 tablespoons oil
1/2 pound pork, (or beef) minced

2 tablespoons dark soy sauce
1 teaspoon chili paste with garlic
1/2 cup chicken stock

Soak vermicelli in boiling water to cover. Let stand 20 minutes. Drain. Cut into thirds. Set aside. Heat oil in wok. Stir fry pork to separate grains of the meat, about 1 minute. Add vermicelli. Blend well. Add soy sauce, chili paste with garlic, and stock. Cook on high heat about 2 to 3 minutes, stirring constantly.

Note: Chili paste w/garlic is available at Asian markets. I make my own with red chili peppers and a garlic clove, both crushed and heated in oil.

"Had a class with Madame Wong in Los Angeles - her recipe!"

Pat Wong   **Taft High School, Taft, CA**

PORK AND BROCCOLI STIR-FRY

Serves 6

1 pound boneless pork loin
1 bunch fresh broccoli
1 red or green bell pepper, seeded and
   cut into thin strips
3/4 cup chicken broth
1 tablespoon cornstarch
2 tablespoons oyster-flavored sauce

1 tablespoon soy sauce
1/8 teaspoon ground ginger
1 tablespoon vegetable oil
1 clove garlic, minced
1/2 cup fresh mushrooms, sliced
1/4 cup green onions, sliced
hot cooked rice

Partially freeze pork; slice across grain into 1/4" slices. Clean broccoli; slice stalks into 1/4" slices; cut off the flowerettes. Set aside with green pepper. Combine chicken broth, cornstarch, oyster-flavored sauce, soy sauce and ginger; set aside. Pour oil around top of preheated wok to cover sides. Heat oil over medium-high heat. Add pork, broccoli stalks, pepper and garlic; stir-fry 4 minutes or until pork is browned. Add broccoli flowerettes, mushrooms and onion; stir-fry 2 minutes. Stir chicken broth mixture; gradually add to wok; mix well. Cook 3 minutes or until thickened and bubbly, stirring constantly. Serve over hot, cooked rice.

National Pork Producers Council   **Des Molnes, IA**

CHASU

Serves 6 - 8   **CHINA**

1/2 cup soy sauce   *4 tablespoons catsup*
2 tablespoon sugar   *1 clove garlic, chopped*
1/2 teaspoon molasses   *4 pounds pork loin roast*

Make a sauce with soy sauce, sugar, molasses, catsup and garlic, Cut pork roast into 1 ½" x 1½" x 5" strips. Marinate in sauce for 2 hours. Bake in 350 degree oven for about 1 hour, basting frequently. Let stand a few minutes before slicing. Serve with hot mustard, if preferred.

Cheryl Sakahara   **Piute Intermediate School, Lancaster, CA**

SWEET AND SOUR PORK

Serves 6   **CHINA**

1 cup lean raw pork, cubed   *3 tablespoons cider vinegar*
*   (about 8 ounces)*   *1/8 teaspoon garlic powder*
2 tablespoons cornstarch   *1 tablespoon cornstarch mixed with 2*
1 tablespoon water   *   tablespoons cold water*
1 tablespoon soy sauce   *1/2 bell pepper, cubed*
oil for deep frying   *1 carrot, cubed*
1/4 cup brown sugar   *1/2 onion, cubed*
2 tablespoons catsup   *2 tablespoons oil*
1/4 cup pineapple juice, reserved   *1 (8 ounce) can pineapple*
*   from canned pineapple*   *   chunks, reserve juice*

Combine cornstarch, water and soy sauce. Marinate pork in mixture for 10 minutes. Heat oil to 375 degrees. Deep fry pork for 10 minutes. Drain. Combine brown sugar, catsup, pineapple juice, vinegar and garlic powder; heat slowly to a boil, stirring constantly. Add cornstarch mixture and continue cooking until mixture thickens. Stir fry vegetables in wok with 2 tablespoons oil for 2 minutes. Add 1/4 cup water; cover and simmer slowly until vegetables are barely tender (2 to 3 minutes). Add pork and pineapple to wok or skillet and heat through. Add sweet and sour sauce; bring to a boil and serve immediately.

"This recipe has a wonderful taste and makes a great main dish."
Rosemary Garland   **Ontario High School, Ontario, CA**

EASY PORK TENDERLOIN

Serves 4

1 - 2 pounds pork tenderloin
2 tablespoons dijon mustard
2 tablespoons brown sugar

1/2 teaspoon fresh ginger, diced
1 teaspoon soy sauce
1/4 cup white wine

Place pork tenderloin on broiling pan. Combine remaining ingredients and brush on tenderloin. Broil 7 minutes per side. Slice thinly on diagonal and serve with steamed rice.

Anne Silveira   **Shasta High School, Redding, CA**

HONG KONG PORK CHOPS

Serves 6

HONG KONG

6 - 8 pork chops
2 tablespoons oil
2 tablespoons lemon juice
1/2 teaspoon ginger
1/4 cup soy sauce

1/4 cup sherry
1 onion, thinly sliced
1 green pepper, cut into strips
1 (4 ounce) can mushrooms, sliced
1 can water chestnuts, sliced

Brown pork chops in oil. Mix lemon juice, ginger, soy sauce and sherry. Place browned pork chops in 9" x 13" baking dish. Top with sliced onions, green pepper, mushrooms and water chestnuts. Pour sauce mixture over the top. Cover with foil and bake at 350 degrees for 1 hour.

"Serve over rice and top with chow mein noodles."

Toni Purtill   **Basic High School, Henderson, NV**

CHINESE ALMOND COOKIES

Makes 6 dozen

CHINA

3 cups flour
1 cup sugar
1 teaspoon soda
1/4 teaspoon salt

1 cup shortening
2 teaspoons almond extract
1 egg, beaten slightly
8 ounces whole blanched almonds

Preheat oven to 350 degrees. Sift flour with sugar, soda and salt. Cut in shortening. Stir in almond extract and egg. Knead until a soft dough is formed. Shape into balls the size of walnuts. Place on baking sheet and flatten slightly. Make a dent about 1/4 inch deep in the center of each cookie and press an almond into the center. Bake for 12 minutes.

"These taste great with a pitcher of hot tea!"

Dotti Jones   **Etiwanda High School, Rancho Cucamonga, CA**

CHINESE CHOCOLATE COOKIES

Makes 3 dozen

CHINA

1 (6 ounce) package chocolate chips
1 (6 ounce) package butterscotch chips

1 can Chinese noodles
1 can salted peanuts

Melt chips in top of a double boiler. Stir in noodles and peanuts. Drop by teaspoonfuls onto cookie sheet. Let stand until set. Then devour!

"Easy, quick and good!"

Gage Hewes   **South Pasadena High School, South Pasadena, CA**

FORTUNE COOKIES

Makes 8   CHINA

1/4 cup cake flour   *2 tablespoons cooking oil*
2 tablespoons sugar   *1 egg white*
1 tablespoon cornstarch   *1 tablespoon water*
dash of salt

Write or type fortunes on small slips of paper before starting. Sift together flour, sugar, cornstarch and salt. Add oil and egg white; stir until smooth. Add water and mix well. Make one cookie at a time: Pour 1 tablespoon batter onto lightly greased skillet or griddle, spreading batter to a 3 1/2 inch circle. Cook over low heat until lightly browned. With wide spatula, life and turn; cook one minute more. Working quickly, place cookie on a pot holder or oven mitt. Place fortune in center; fold cookie in half and fold again over edge of a bowl. Place in muffin pan to cool.

"It's fun to make up your own fortunes!"

Peg DellaZoppa   **Yucca Valley High School, Yucca Valley, CA**

BATA MOCHI (BUTTER RICE CAKES)

Makes 32 squares   JAPAN

5 eggs   *1 (16 ounce) box mochiko*
2 cups sugar   *   (sweet rice flour)*
1 1/2 teaspoons baking powder   *1/2 cup butter or margarine, melted*
3 cups milk   *1 teaspoon vanilla*

Preheat oven to 350 degrees. Beat eggs and sugar until lemon colored. Add the remaining ingredients , beat until smooth. Pour into a 13" x 9" Pyrex baking dish which has been sprayed with vegetable cooking spray. Bake for 1 hour. Cool and cut into 2" x 1" pieces.

"Use a plastic knife to cut the squares so the mochi will not stick to it."

Edna Nagami   **Carr Intermediate School, Santa Ana, CA**

BANGKOK BANANA FRITTERS

Serves 6   THAILAND

6 bananas   *1 cup water*
1 cup coconut, grated (packaged)   *1 teaspoon baking powder*
2 cups crisp rice cereal, crushed   *1/2 teaspoon salt*
2 tablespoons salad oil   *shortening or oil for deep fat frying*
1 cup flour   *powdered sugar*

Peel bananas, cut in half crosswise and score outsides with a fork. Combine coconut and cereal. Roll bananas firmly in coconut and cereal mixture; make sure ends and sides are thoroughly coated. Heat deep fat fryer to 360 degrees. Combine salad oil, flour, water, baking powder and salt into a smooth batter. Dip bananas in batter - fry until nicely browned (do 2 to 3 at a time). Keep warm in a slow oven until the remainder are fried. Sprinkle with powdered sugar before serving.

"If you like bananas - you'll love this recipe!"

Sharron Maurice   **Blythe Middle School, Blythe, CA**

ANZAC BISCUITS

Makes 35   **AUSTRALIA**

1 cup rolled oats
1 cup plain flour, sifted
1 cup sugar
3/4 cup coconut

1/2 cup butter
2 tablespoons dark Karo corn syrup
1/2 teaspoon baking soda
1 tablespoon boiling water

Combine oats, flour, sugar and coconut. Combine butter and Karo syrup; stir over gentle heat until melted. Mix soda with boiling water; add to melted butter mixture; stir into dry ingredients. Take teaspoonfuls of mixture and place on lightly greased oven trays; allow room for spreading. Cook in slow oven, 300 degrees for 20 minutes. Loosen from pan while still warm, then cool on trays.

"These are a traditional Australia biscuit (cookie) served on Anzac Day, April 25, a Memorial-type holiday in honor of the Australian and New Zealand Army Corps."

Robyn Nadell   Bernardo Yorba Middle School, Yorba Linda, CA

PAVLOVA

Serves 8   **AUSTRALIA**

6 egg whites
pinch of cream of tartar
2 cups sugar
1 1/2 teaspoons vinegar
1 1/2 teaspoons vanilla

cool whip
kiwi, sliced
strawberries, sliced
pineapple slices

Beat egg whites with a pinch of cream of tartar until thick. Gradually beat in sifted sugar, one tablespoon at a time , then vinegar and vanilla. Cover a pizza tray with foil and grease lightly. Spoon meringue in a circle onto the tray; bake in a very slow oven, 250 degrees for 1 hour in an electric oven or 1 1/2 hours in a gas oven. Turn oven off and let pavlova sit in oven until completely cooled. To serve: spread with cool whip and top with kiwi, strawberries and pineapple slices. Serve in pie slices.

"My long time pen pal finally came to California and we met. She made this dessert at her farewell dinner."

Sheryl Holtz   Redwood Intermediate School, Thousand Oaks, CA

EASTERN EUROPE

Poland
Russia

Russia and Poland have many nationalities and therefore have a vast variety of foods and traditions surrounding them. Not all of its people eat borscha, kasha and beef stroganov. While the northerners eat blackwheat grown in their area, the easterners are influenced by Oriental flavors, and the Baltic peoples have adopted many Scandinavian traditions.

Preoccupation with food is constant in classic Russian literature. One of Chekhov's heroes strikes a universal theme when he complained that he had never been able to accomplish anything because the moment he set to work his concentration was broken by thoughts of food – even the image of a boiled potato was enough to distract him for a day!

€ASTERN €UROPE

MUSHROOM A LA RUSSE

Serves 6   RUSSIA

2 pounds mushrooms
juice of 1/2 lemon
2 cans condensed cream of
    mushroom soup
1 tablespoon butter

1/3 cup heavy cream
1/3 cup sour cream
salt and pepper
1 package puff pastry, prepared
    according to package directions

Wash mushrooms; drain and slice. Cover with water; add lemon juice and simmer until mushrooms are tender, about 10 minutes. Drain. Combine soup, butter, heavy cream and sour cream. Heat until bubbly. Fold in sliced mushrooms. Season to taste with salt and pepper. Serve over prepared puff pastry.

Gloria Francuch   **Carpinteria High School, Carpinteria, CA**

PIROGHI (STUFFED PASTRIES)

Makes 3 dozen   RUSSIA

3 tablespoons yeast
1 tablespoon sugar
1 cup flour
6 eggs, beaten

1 cup sour cream
1 cup margarine or shortening, melted
1 teaspoon salt
4 1/4 cups flour

Filling: (any of the following)
mashed potatoes
mashed beans

1 cup cottage cheese mixed with 1 egg
pumpkin seasoned with sugar

Mix eggs, sour cream and margarine or shortening in a bowl; set aside. Dissolve yeast and sugar in 1 cup lukewarm water. Let rise for 10 minutes. Add 2 cups flour to egg mixture and mix with a wooden spoon. Add yeast mixture and remaining flour; shape dough into small balls. Start rolling the balls in order shaped. Fill with favorite filling, pinch closed and let rise for 45 minutes. Bake at 400 degrees for 10 to 12 minutes.

"A great accompaniment to a meal or as a snack."

Tanya Goosev   **Reedley High School, CA**

POTATO PANCAKES (PLACKI Z KARTOFLI)

Serves 4   POLAND

2 cups raw potatoes, grated
2 tablespoons flour
2 eggs, well beaten

1 teaspoon salt
1 teaspoon sugar

Grate potatoes and cover with water to keep from turning brown. Drain well. Add remaining ingredients and beat well. With spoon, drop mixture on hot griddle and spread as thinly as possibly. Fry on both sides.

Kathie Baczynski   **Mt. Carmel High School, San Diego, CA**

POLISH POTATO SOUP

Serves 6   **POLAND**

1 tablespoon butter or margarine
1 pound kielbasa (polish sausage)
1 onion, chopped
2 cups celery and leaves
2 cups carrots, sliced
5 cups water
1 teaspoon salt

1 bay leaf
1/2 teaspoon thyme leaves
2 beef bouillon cubes
2 tablespoons white vinegar
3 - 4 cups potatoes, cubed
4 cups cabbage, shredded

Melt butter in large kettle; saute kielbasa, onion and celery until tender. Add all ingredients except potatoes and cabbage. Cook 1 hour, covered. Add potatoes and cabbage and cook 1 hour more, covered. Serve with hot bread or crackers.

"A favorite at Lenton Soup & Salad Suppers at our church."

Deanne Moody   **Monte Vista High School, Spring Valley, CA**

TRADITIONAL MATZO BALLS

Serves 8   **RUSSIA**

2 tablespoons chicken fat, melted
2 eggs, slightly beaten
1/2 cup matzo meal

1 teaspoon salt
2 tablespoons water

Mix chicken fat and eggs together. Add matzo meal and salt. When well blended, add water and mix; shape into 8 balls. Cover mixing bowl and refrigerate 20 minutes. Using a 3 quart pot, bring salted water to a boil. Reduce flame and drop matzo balls into slightly bubbling water. Cover pot and let cook for 35 minutes. Drain water after matzo balls are cooked. Serve in chicken soup.

Marlene Pollock   **Norte Vista High School, Riverside, CA**

STUFFED CABBAGE ROLLS (HOLUBKY)

Makes 40 - 50   **POLAND**

2 cups rice, uncooked
3 - 4 medium-sized heads cabbage
3 onions, chopped
4 cloves garlic, minced (optional)
1/2 cup margarine

2 pounds ground beef
salt to taste
pepper to taste
1/4 cup parsley, minced
1 can tomato soup

Cook rice according to package directions but reducing cooking time to 10 minutes; drain and cool. Core cabbages and parboil in boiling water, removing leaves as they soften but are firm enough to roll; cool. Trim the thick ridge on back of leaves to make it easier for rolling. Saute onions and garlic in margarine until golden brown. Combine with meat, rice, salt and pepper and parsley; mix well. Spread each cabbage leaf, beginning at thick end, with meat mixture; fold over two opposite ends and roll. Place rolls in a roasting pan or Dutch oven. Spread with tomato soup and cover cabbages with water. Bake, covered, at 325 degrees for about 2 hours or until lightly browned and tender.VARIATIONS: Ground pork can be used for part of the meat. Sauerkraut can be layered between rolls."

"This is our traditional holiday meal. To make it easier, I cook the rice and cabbage the night before."

Millie Deeton   **Ayala High School, Chino, CA**

RUSSIAN GOULASH

Serves 4   **RUSSIA**

1 pound lean ground beef	*1 can mushrooms, sliced*
2 onions, diced	*6 cans beef broth*
1 small green pepper, chopped	*salt & pepper to taste*
1 clove garlic, minced	*1 package egg noodles*
1 tablespoon paprika	*cooking sherry (optional)*
1/2 teaspoon caraway	*sour cream*
1 (8 ounce) can stewed tomatoes, w/liquid	

Brown and drain beef. Add onions, green pepper, garlic, paprika and caraway. Then add tomatoes, mushrooms, broth, salt and pepper. Simmer 30 minutes. Ten minutes before serving, add egg noodles. Just prior to serving add sherry, if desired. Garnish with a blob of sour cream.

"This recipe is actually from a Yugoslavian woman."

Jan Schulenburg   **Irvine High School, Irvine, CA**

LOW FAT STROGANOFF

Serves 4   **RUSSIA**

1/2 onion, sliced	*1 can low-fat cream of mushroom*
1/2 pound mushrooms, sliced	*soup*
1 tablespoon water	*1 tablespoon water*
1 teaspoon garlic powder	*brown rice or noodles, prepared*
1 pound lean ground beef or ground turkey	

Saute onion and mushrooms in 1 tablespoon water with the garlic powder. Add ground meat and brown. Add soup and sour cream. Cook on low to medium heat until it bubbles (about 15 minutes). Serve on brown rice or noodles.

"Low fat recipe!"

Pam Fecchino   **Cimarron-Memorial High School, Las Vegas, NV**

BEEF STROGANOFF

Serves 6 - 8   **RUSSIA**

2 pounds round steak, trimmed
*   of fat and gristle*
1/2 cup flour
1 1/2 teaspoons salt
1 teaspoon paprika
1/2 cup onion, chopped
1/4 cup salad oil or non-stick
*   cooking spray*

1 can consomme
1/2 can water
1 bay leaf
1/2 teaspoon thyme
1/2 teaspoon oregano
1 (4 ounce) can mushrooms, or
*   sauteed fresh mushroom*
1 cup sour cream (fat free okay)

Cut steak into bite-sized pieces (cuts more easily if slightly frozen). Combine flour, salt and paprika and coat meat. Brown meat with onions in oil or use cooking spray to reduce fat. Add consomme, water and herbs; cover and simmer until meat is tender, adding a little more water if necessary. Just before serving, stir in mushrooms and sour cream. Heat and serve over hot rice or noodles.

"The original recipe was in the 1958 edition of 'Parent's Magazine Cookbook'. I add 2 tablespoons cooking sherry with the sour cream and mushrooms. A favorite for holiday and company meals."

Barbara Warren   **Colton High School, Colton, CA**

CHICKEN KIEV

Serves 8   **RUSSIA**

1/2 cup + 4 tablespoons butter or
*   margarine, softened, divided*
2 tablespoons lemon juice
1 tablespoon + 1/2 teaspoon garlic
*   seasoning, or to taste, divided*
1 tablespoon dried parsley
8 boneless chicken breasts
2 eggs
2 1/2 cups milk, divided

2 cups dry bread crumbs
4 tablespoons butter or margarine
4 tablespoons flour
1 teaspoon salt
1/2 teaspoon pepper
4 - 5 drops hot sauce (or to taste)
fresh parsley, for garnish
red pepper strips, for garnish

Make butter logs: mix together 1/2 cup butter, lemon juice, 1 tablespoon garlic seasoning and dried parsley. Shape into small logs about 1 inch long and 1/2 inch in diameter. Place on a plate and put into the freezer until very cold. Meanwhile, flatten chicken breasts between pieces of wax paper. Remove butter logs from freezer and place 1 log on top of a chicken breast. Roll up and secure with toothpicks. Mix together eggs and 1/2 cup milk. Pour into a shallow bowl. Place bread crumbs in another shallow bowl. Dip chicken rolls in the egg/milk mixture and then into the bread crumbs. Coat thoroughly. Place on a baking tray and return to the freezer for approximately 30 minutes so that the butter logs are thoroughly chilled. Bake at 350 degrees for 40 to 45 minutes or until chicken is done and bread crumbs are browned. Meanwhile, make a white sauce: melt 4 tablespoons butter in a saucepan over low heat. Add the flour, salt, 1/2 teaspoon garlic seasoning, salt, pepper and hot sauce, stirring until blended and smooth. Cook for about 1 minute; do not brown. Remove from heat. Add 2 cups milk gradually, stirring constantly. Return saucepan to heat; cook just until bubbly, stirring constantly.

Serve: Remove toothpicks from the chicken. Place one or two Chicken Kiev rolls on a plate and pour white sauce over the top. Garnish with fresh parsley and strips of red pepper.

"When you cut into the Chicken Kiev logs, the butter/garlic mixture bursts free and adds such flavor to the meal!"

Dotti Jones   **Etiwanda High School, Rancho Cucamonga, CA**

RUSSIAN CHICKEN WITH GOOSEBERRY SAUCE

Serves 4   **RUSSIA**

4 broiler-fryer chicken quarters
1 teaspoon salt
1/4 teaspoon thyme
1/4 teaspoon rosemary
1/4 teaspoon oregano
1 (16 ounce) can gooseberries
    in light syrup

2 tablespoons flour
2 tablespoons butter
2 tablespoons white wine
1 3/4 cups chicken broth, heated

Mix together salt, thyme, rosemary and oregano; rub mixture on chicken quarters and arrange on rack in baking pan. Bake at 375 degrees for about 45 minutes or until fork can be inserted in chicken with ease. Remove chicken to warm platter. Pour off fat and reserve remainder of pan drippings. Drain gooseberries well, reserving 1/4 cup of the light syrup. Place flour in ungreased frypan and cook, stirring over medium heat for about 2 minutes. Add butter and stir until melted. Add gooseberry syrup and wine to hot broth and slowly pour into frypan, stirring until thickened and bubbly. Add reserved pan drippings and gooseberries; then add chicken quarters, spooning gooseberries gently over all. Simmer about 3 minutes.

National Broiler Council   **Columbia, SC**

RUSSIAN TEA CAKES

Makes 5 - 6 dozen   **RUSSIA**

1 pound butter or margarine
1 cup powdered sugar
4 cups flour

3 tablespoons vanilla
2 cups nuts, chopped

Cream butter and sugar. Add flour, vanilla and chopped nuts. Shape in balls the size of a walnut (about 1") being careful not to overhandle dough. Bake in a moderate oven, 350 degrees, for about 15 minutes until lightly browned. Cool slightly. Roll in powdered sugar once or twice.

"This is a truly international cookie. I have seen this same recipe called Mexican Wedding Cakes and also the Americanized name, Snowball Holiday cookies. These are very attractive when they are placed next to a dark cookie like brownies on a tray of holiday cookies."

Maggy Flath   ' **Nevada Union High School, Grass Valley, CA**

EUROPE

Austria
England
Europe
France
Germany
Greece
Ireland
Italy
Scotland
Spain
Switzerland

"The grand cuisine" of France which can be found in most of the famous restaurants around the world; the myriad pasta and sauce recipes of Italy; the savory Hellenic cuisine of Greece; and the hearty traditional German cookery has resisted outside influences. Such are the majestic cultures that give European cuisine its depth and splendor.

EUROPE

FRENCH HOT CHOCOLATE

Serves 10   **FRANCE**

2 ounces unsweetened chocolate
1/2 cup water
3/4 cup sugar
1/2 teaspoon salt (optional)

1/2 cup heavy cream, (whipped
    to 1 cup)
hot milk

In a saucepan over low heat, melt unsweetened chocolate squares and water until thick, stirring constantly. Add sugar and salt and continue cooking, approximately 4 minutes; cool. Fold in whipped whipping cream and store mixture in an air-tight container in the refrigerator until ready to make hot chocolate. To serve: Heat milk to 150 degrees, just below scalding. Place 1 heaping tablespoon chocolate mixture in each mug and add enough hot milk to fill mug; stir well. Serve immediately and enjoy!

"Well worth the extra effort and a wonderful treat for your chocolate loving friends!"
Debbie Sullivan   **Silverado High School, Henderson, NV**

PESTO DIP

Makes 2 cups   **ITALY**

1 cup mayonnaise
1 cup sour cream
1 (10 ounce) package spinach
1/3 cup parmesan cheese, grated

1/4 cup walnut pieces
1 teaspoon dried basil
1/4 teaspoon salt
1 garlic clove, crushed

In blender or food processor, blend all ingredients until almost smooth. Cover and chill.

"This is very popular - especially served with vegetables."
Karen Talley   **Santa Maria High School, Santa Maria, CA**

HOMEMADE SALAMI

Makes Four 4" logs   **ITALY**

4 pounds inexpensive ground beef
1/4 cup curing salt
4 tablespoons liquid smoke

3 teaspoons garlic powder
3 teaspoons ground pepper

Thoroughly mix all ingredients and chill for 24 hours. Divide mixture into fourths. Shape each into a compact 8 inch log. Put on a 12" x 18" piece of nylon net. Roll up tightly. Tie ends with string. Bake on a broiler pan 4 hours at 225 degrees. Remove from oven and take off net. Pat dry with paper towel. Cool slightly. Roll in foil and freeze or refrigerate.

"This is a favorite with the men in my family. Great with cheese and crackers."

Laury White   **Baldwin Park High School, Baldwin Park, CA**

BREADED CAULIFLOWER

Serves 4 - 6   **ITALY**

1 head cauliflower   *2 tablespoons cornstarch*
2 eggs   *1/4 cup Parmesan cheese, grated*
1/4 teaspoon salt   *oil for deep frying*
2 cups cracker crumbs

Separate cauliflower into bite-sized pieces and parboil in salted water; let cool. Beat together eggs and salt. Combine cracker crumbs, cornstarch and Parmesan cheese. Dip cauliflower into egg and roll in cracker crumb mixture. Deep fry until golden brown. Serve immediately.

Loretta Salau   **Foothill High School, Bakersfield, CA**

SPANAKOPITAS

Makes 42   **GREECE**

2 small onions, diced   *1/3 cup Parmesan cheese, grated*
2 tablespoons olive oil   *1/8 teaspoon pepper*
1 (10 ounce) package frozen chopped   *approximately 1/3 pound phyllo dough*
  spinach, thawed and drained   *1/2 cup butter or margarine, melted*
1 egg

Preheat oven to 425 degrees. In 2 quart saucepan over medium heat, cook onion in olive oil until tender, stirring occasionally. Remove from heat; stir in spinach, egg, cheese and pepper. With knife, cut phyllo dough lengthwise into 2 inch wide strips. Place strips on waxed paper then cover with slightly damp towel. Brush top of one strip of phyllo with melted butter; place 1 teaspoonful spinach mixture at short end of strip. Fold one corner of strip diagonally over filling so the short edge meets the long edge, forming a right angle (triangle). Continue folding over at right angles until you reach the end of the strip to form a triangular shape package. Repeat with remaining phyllo strips and spinach filling. Place packages, seam side down, in 15-1/2" x 10-1/2" jelly roll pan; brush with melted butter. Bake triangles 15 minutes, or until golden brown. Serve hot.

"Terrific appetizers!"

Leslie Rodden   **San Gorgonio High School, San Bernardino, CA**

MONTEREY FRENCH BREAD

Serves 12 - 15   **FRANCE**

1 loaf French bread (baguette)   *1/2 cup Parmesan cheese*
1 cup mayonnaise   *1/2 teaspoon worcestershire sauce*
1/2 cup green onion, chopped

Slice bread into 1" rounds. Mix together remaining ingredients and spread on each slice. Brown under broiler until golden in color, about 2 minutes.

"My Aunt Jennie Fetterly brings this to our family gatherings, and it's always gone in a flash!"

Carol Delap   **Golden West High School, Visalia, CA**

GRANDMA NANCY MESSINA'S EGG PANCAKES

Serves 6 - 8   **ITALY**

Sweet sauce:
1 large yellow onion
1 tablespoon olive oil
1 large can crushed tomatoes or
    whole garden tomatoes

1 small can of water
3 tablespoons sweet basil, fresh or dried
1 tablespoon sugar
1 tablespoon olive oil

Pancake batter:
6 eggs
1 cup Italian bread crumbs
1 cup Romano cheese, grated
1/2 cup water

1 teaspoon salt
1 teaspoon pepper
3 tablespoons olive oil

First, make the Sweet Sauce: brown the onion in 1 tablespoon olive oil. Add the crushed tomatoes, tomato paste, water, basil and sugar; let simmer for 30 minutes.

To make pancakes: break eggs into bowl and scramble with fork or whisk. Add the cheese, bread crumbs, water, salt and pepper. Mix with fork or whisk until blended. In a hot frying pan (non stick is best) add about 3 tablespoons oil. When oil is hot, add pancake batter to form small size pancakes. Let cook until brown on one side, then flip pancake to brown on the other side. Repeat process until all the batter is finished.

Add browned pancakes to sauce pan with sweet sauce, stacking pancakes on top of each other in the sauce. Let cook on simmer for about 30 minutes until sauce has soaked into pancakes. Serve hot or cold, by themselves or in a sandwich.

Cathy Francois   **Carlsbad High School, Carlsbad, CA**

AUNTIE ALICE'S SCONES

Makes 1 dozen   **SCOTLAND**

3 cups flour
1 tablespoon baking powder
1/2 teaspoon baking soda
1/2 teaspoon salt
1/2 cup sugar
3/4 cup butter, cut up (1 1/2 cubes)
1/2 cup raisins

1/2 cup walnuts, chopped (optional)
1 cup buttermilk
12 sugar cubes (use more if you
    make more than 12 scones)
1/2 cup orange juice
1 tablespoon whipping cream or milk

Preheat oven to 400 degrees. Sift together dry ingredients and cut in butter with a pastry cutter. Stir in raisins and walnuts. Make a well in the center. Pour in buttermilk and mix into a round dough ball. Place on floured board and pat into 3/4 inch thick circle. Cut into triangles or desired shape. Place on a greased cooking sheet. Take 1 sugar cube, dip in orange juice and press into center of each biscuit. Brush top with milk or cream. Bake for 14 to 18 minutes. Serve warm with preserves, jam or butter.

"My good friend, Marsha Norton, served this for a Christmas Tea. Everyone said they were the best scones they had ever tasted. I agree."

Marianne Traw   **Ball Junior High School, Anaheim, CA**

DAKOTA-STYLE KUCHEN

Serves Many   **GERMANY**

1 loaf frozen bread dough or your own   *1 cup cream*
*   recipe for sweet yeast bread*   *1/2 cup sugar*
2 cups fresh fruit, thinly sliced, or   *3 eggs*
*   dehydrated dried fruit*   *1 teaspoon cinnamon*

Thaw frozen dough (if using) and allow to rise once. Divide dough into fourths. Roll each quarter out into 9" circle and pat into pie pan leaving 1/2" rim all around. Place 1/2 cup desired fruit into each pie pan. Prepare a custard by whipping cream, then adding sugar, eggs and cinnamon. Pour equal amounts over each kuchen. Allow to set about 1/2 hour. Bake at 400 degrees for 20 to 25 minutes. Serve hot, warm or cool. Store in bags in refrigerator.

"A recipe prepared by German families, especially my own - even now that we're far away from 'Dakota'."

Charlotte Heitzmann   **Mariposa County High School, Mariposa, CA**

CHEESY ONION FLATBREAD

Serves 8   **ITALY**

1/4 cup Parmesan cheese, grated   *1/4 teaspoon dried basil leaves*
1/4 cup mayonnaise   *1/4 teaspoon dried oregano leaves*
1/2 cup green onions, chopped   *1 (11 ounce) can Pillsbury Refrigerated*
1/2 teaspoon garlic powder   *   Soft Breadsticks*

Heat oven to 350 degrees. In a medium bowl, combine all ingredients except breadsticks. Mix well; set aside. Remove dough from can. Separate into 8 coils. DO NOT unroll breadsticks. Place coils on an ungreased cookie sheet. Press each coil into a 4" circle. Spread 1 tablespoon cheese mixture on each circle to within 1/4" of edge. Bake at 350 degrees for 13 - 18 minutes. Serve warm.

"Great change from garlic French bread."

Adrienne Bahn   **Lee Junior High School, Woodland, CA**

PEPPERONI TWISTS

Serves 8 - 10   **ITALY**

1 loaf frozen bread dough, thawed   *1/2 cup pepperoni, chopped*
2 tablespoons butter or margarine,   *1/2 cup mozzarella cheese, grated*
*   melted*   *1/2 cup Parmesan cheese, grated*
1 teaspoon garlic powder

Roll dough into a 10" x 12" rectangle. Brush dough with 1/2 of the melted butter. Top with garlic powder, pepperoni, mozzarella and half of the Parmesan. Fold dough in half, lengthwise. Seal edges. With a thread or sharp knife, divide dough into 12 or more pieces. Gently pull and twist each piece. Place 2 inches apart on greased cookie sheet. Brush with remaining butter and top with Parmesan cheese. Let rise 30 minutes to one hour. Bake at 375 degrees for 12 to 15 minutes or until golden brown.

"Great snack with kid appeal!"

Nanci Burkhart   **Hueneme High School, Oxnard, CA**

FOCACCIA BREAD

Serves 6 - 8   **ITALY**

1 tablespoon yeast	*2 1/2 cups flour*
1 cup warm water	*garlic, diced (desired amount for topping)*
1 teaspoon salt	*basil (desired amount for topping)*
1 tablespoon olive oil	*oregano (desired amount for topping)*

Dissolves yeast in warm water. Add salt, olive oil and 2 cups flour and beat well. Knead in remaining 1/2 cup flour . Form a smooth ball and spread with shortening. Cover and let rise until doubled. Divide and form dough into 2 flat rounds. Place on a cookie sheet. Rub the top of each loaf with olive oil and press diced garlic in each. Sprinkle with basil and oregano. Bake in a preheated 400 degree oven for 15 to 20 minutes, or until golden brown.

"This is an ancient poorman's bread, which later, with added toppings, became pizza! No butter is needed with these flavors!"

Lynda Waugh   **San Marcos Junior High School, San Marcos, CA**

GAZPACHO

Serves 4   **SPAIN**

1 clove garlic	*4 eggs*
4 sprigs watercress or parsley	*1/4 cup lemon juice*
1 medium onion, chopped	*1/4 cup olive oil*
1 cucumber, chopped	*1/8 teaspoon salt*
3 tomatoes, peeled and chopped	*1/8 teaspoon red pepper*
1 green bell pepper, seeded and chopped	*3/4 cup tomato juice*

In an electric blender, blend garlic, watercress, onion, cucumber, tomatoes, green bell peppers and eggs until well blended. Add the remaining ingredients and blend to mix only. Transfer to a glass bowl; cover and chill. Serve with additional chopped cucumbers, sweet onion, tomatoes and bread cubes each in it's own small bowl.

NOTE: Can be made up to one day ahead.

"Very refreshing on a hot summer day."

Dorothy Alves   **Grace Davis High School, Modesto, CA**

Tomato Pesto Lasagna, Page 79

Chicken Milano, Page 75

Viennese Almond Torte, Page 90

EASY VICHYSSOISE

Serves 6   FRANCE

2 (10 ounce) cans condensed chicken
    broth
1 teaspoon celery salt
1 teaspoon onion powder

1 individual package French's instant
    mashed potatoes
2 cups half & half

Easy Vichyssoise: Put broth in saucepan; add seasonings, bring to a boil. Add potatoes and stir out all lumps. Blend in half & half and allow to cool. Refrigerate and serve very cold.

"This is so easy and delicious, you'll never use another recipe. I like it hot too!"
Marilyn Tam   **Orange Glen High School, Escondido, CA**

FRENCH ONION SOUP

Serves 6   FRANCE

6 large yellow onions, thinly sliced
1/2 cup butter
2 (10 1/2 ounce) cans condensed
    beef broth
1 soup can water

1 soup can dry white wine
6 slices French bread, toasted,
    about 1" thick
3/4 cup Parmesan or Gruyere cheese,
    freshly grated (if possible)

Saute onions in butter until lightly browned. Add broth, water and wine. Simmer until onions are tender. Spoon soup into earthenware or other ovenproof bowls. Top each serving bowl with toasted French bread that has been cut to fit top of bowl. Sprinkle with grated cheese. Broil until cheese has melted and is golden brown.

"A special cold weather treat that is super-easy to prepare."
Linda Paskins   **Cordova High School, Rancho Cordova, CA**

15 MINUTE MINESTRONE SOUP

Serves 6 to 8   ITALY

2 chicken breasts, cut into 1 inch pieces
1 (14 1/2 ounce) can chicken broth
1 (15 ounce) can kidney beans
1 cup frozen mixed vegetables
1/2 cup onion, chopped
1/2 cup pasta shells, uncooked

1/2 teaspoon basil
1/2 teaspoon thyme
1/4 teaspoon pepper
1 (14 1/2 ounce) can stewed
    Italian tomatoes

Stir all ingredients in saucepan except chicken. Simmer, covered 10 minutes. Add chicken and bring to a boil. Boil 4 to 5 minutes, or until chicken loses pink color.

"This is an excellent recipe for when you are in a hurry and time is at a premium."
Roberta S. Priestley   **Alhambra High School, Alhambra, CA**

ITALIAN TORTELLINI SOUP

Serves 4 - 6   ITALY

1 pound Italian sausage or Jimmy Dean
    mild sausage
2 cloves garlic, minced
1 small onion, diced
1/2 cup water
3 cups chicken broth
1/2 cup white wine
1 (16 ounce) can Italian stewed
    tomatoes, chopped, including juice

1 (8 ounce) can tomato sauce
1 cup carrots, sliced thin
1 teaspoon basil leaves, dried
1/2 teaspoon oregano
2 medium zucchini, sliced
1 (8 ounce) package tortellini, your
    choice of flavor
2 tablespoons parsley

In a soup pot, brown and cook sausage, garlic and onion. Add rest of ingredients, except zucchini, tortellini and parsley. Simmer for 30 minutes. Stir in zucchini, tortellini and parsley. Simmer another 30 minutes. (Add more broth if it needs to be thinner.)

"Serve with freshly grated Parmesan cheese and a basket of French bread."

Gail McAuley   **Lincoln High School, Stockton, CA**

CIOPPINO

Serves 8   ITALY

1 cup onion, chopped
1 cup parsley, chopped
1 cup celery, chopped
2 large cloves garlic, minced
1/2 cup olive oil
2 (2 1/2#) cans stewed tomatoes

4 crabs, cleaned, cracked and broken
    into sections
12 to 18 clams, in the shell
2 pounds shrimp, peeled
1 pound scallops

1 can tomato paste
1 teaspoon Italian seasoning
1/2 teaspoon oregano
salt and pepper, to taste
4 cups water
salt and pepper, to taste

2 pounds white fish, cut in chunks
squid, abalone, oysters and any other
    assorted seafood to cook's choice
2 cups dry red wine

In a large, deep stainless steel soup pot, cook onion, parsley, celery and garlic in olive oil until they turn transparent. Add tomatoes, tomato paste, seasonings and water. Simmer for 30 minutes, with lid on. Add crab, clams, fish, scallops, other shellfish and wine. Cover and simmer for 15 to 20 minutes. If too tomatoey, add a cup or so of additional water. Serve in large soup bowls with warm sourdough bread.

"This is a family favorite on our vacations along the north coast."

Kay Linberger   **Tokay High School, Lodi, CA**

BASQUE VEGETABLE SOUP

Serves 6 - 8   FRANCE

1 pound white beans
1/2 pound dry peas
1 meaty hambone
3 bay leaves
1 onion
whole cloves
5 - 6 potatoes
4 carrots, sliced

4 turnips, diced
5 leeks, sliced
2 - 3 garlic cloves, minced
1 teaspoon thyme
12 sausages
1 small cabbage, shredded
Swiss cheese, grated (for topping)

Soak beans and peas overnight. Drain and rinse. In a large pan, cook beans and peas, hambone, 2 bay leaves, 1 onion studded with whole cloves and 3 quarts of water for about 1 - 2 hours, until tender. Drain and reserve liquid, setting beans, peas and hambone aside.(When hambone has cooled, remove meat and discard bone.) In bean liquid, cook potatoes, carrots, turnips, leeks, garlic, thyme, and remaining bay leaf for 15 to 20 minutes. Meanwhile lightly brown sausages. When vegetables are tender, add beans and peas, ham, cabbage, sausages and cook 10 minutes, until cabbage is cooked. Sprinkle with Swiss cheese to serve.

"Bakersfield people love Basque food. Soup is just the first course of many!"
Judy Betz   **Greenfield Junior High School, Bakersfield, CA**

PEPERONATA

Serves 6   ITALY

1/4 cup olive oil
1 large onion, thinly sliced
1 large red bell pepper, thinly sliced
1 large green bell pepper, thinly sliced

1 large yellow bell pepper, thinly sliced
1 tablespoon balsamic or red wine
* vinegar*
salt & pepper to taste

Heat oil in a heavy, large skillet over medium-low heat. Add onions and bell peppers and saute until onions and bell peppers are very tender, about 40 minutes. Mix in vinegar. Season to taste with salt and pepper. Serve hot, warm or at room temperature.

"This is a great make-ahead vegetable. It can also be cooked for only about 5 minutes, and served as a salad after chilling."
Jan Hirth   **Saddleback High School, Santa Ana, CA**

CREAMY POLENTA

Serves 5   ITALY

2 cups chicken broth
2 cups milk
1 cup Polenta (found with cornmeal &
* cereals in market)*

1 cup Tileme, jack or cheddar cheese,
* grated*
1/2 cube butter
salt to taste

Bring milk and chicken broth to a boil. Add polenta slowly. After polenta is mixed well, add cheese and butter and season to taste. Cook until creamy and thick, about 40 minutes. Use a heat diffuser under pot if possible.

"This recipe is often prepared by a good friend and served with a meat dish. It is an excellent substitute for potatoes or pasta with the main course."

Dianne Sheats   **Gridley High School, Gridley, CA**

ROSTI (SWISS POTATO CAKE)

Serves 4   SWITZERLAND

2 pounds potatoes (about 4 large)   *2 tablespoons oil*
2 tablespoons butter or margarine   *1/2 teaspoon salt*

Drop potatoes into boiling water to cover and boil about 10 minutes. Drain. When cool, peel; cover with plastic wrap and refrigerate for 1 hour. Grate them into long strips. In a heavy, 10 inch teflon skillet, heat 1 tablespoon butter or margarine and 1 tablespoon oil and salt. Fry about 8 to 10 minutes or until golden brown. Place on a plate over the skillet, invert onto plate; add remaining oil and butter or margarine in skillet to melt. Slide the potatoes back into the skillet and fry about 6 to 8 minutes. Flip the potato cake out and serve at once.

"My parents and I have loved eating Rosti in Switzerland! Now, we can enjoy this specialty in our own homes!"

Gail Hurt   **Estancia High School, Costa Mesa, CA**

GRANDMA'S RED CABBAGE

Serves 6   GERMANY

1 large head red cabbage   *3/4 cup sugar*
1/4 cup water   *1 apple, finely chopped*
1/2 cup vinegar   *1/2 cup shortening*

Shred cabbage. Bring water, vinegar and sugar to a boil. Add cabbage, apple and shortening. Reduce heat and simmer for about one hour.

"This is a wonderful German side dish my grandmother would make on special occasions."

Joanne Montoy   **Esperanza High School, Anaheim, CA**

ZUCCHINI PESTO

Serves 4   ITALY

1 small handful fresh basil   *1 cup low-fat ricotta cheese*
1 clove garlic (or more to taste)   *salt and pepper to taste*
3 medium zucchini, chunked and   *1 tablespoon parmesan cheese,*
*   steamed (reserve liquid)*   *   grated (optional)*
1 to 2 tablespoons olive oil

Toss basil and garlic into a blender or food processor and process until finely chopped. Add remaining ingredients and puree until smooth. Adjust seasonings and add reserved zucchini liquid if sauce is too thick (chicken stock may be used - it will give a richer flavor). Toss with warm pasta, preferably angel hair or thin spaghetti.

"This is a great way to use zucchini that is so plentiful during the season. Freezes great. This is also a great way to get kids to eat zucchini."

Vicki Giannetti   **Foothill High School, Sacramento, CA**

RISOTTO (ITALIAN RICE)

Serves 4   **ITALY**

3 tablespoons butter   *1 medium carrot, grated*
2 tablespoons olive oil   *1/2 cup petite peas, frozen*
1 onion, chopped   *Parmesan, domestic Romano or*
2 cloves garlic, minced   *Asiago cheese, freshly grated*
1 cup Italian rice (risotto)   *salt, to taste*
3 cups hot chicken broth   *pepper, to taste*

Melt butter; add olive oil and saute onion and garlic until tender and golden. Add rice and cook, stirring constantly, until opaque, about 3 minutes. Stir in one fourth of hot broth stirring until absorbed. Continue adding broth in one fourth quantities until all broth is absorbed. Stir in grated carrot, peas and grated cheese. Add salt and pepper to taste.

Variations: add cut up chicken, shrimp and/or other vegetables.

"This recipe is a delicious accompaniment for chicken and fish."

Sharon Turner   **El Dorado High School, Placentia, CA**

GNOCCHI

Serves 5 - 6   **ITALY**

7 small potatoes   *4 quarts water*
1 egg   *spaghetti sauce, of your choice*
2 1/2 cups all purpose flour   *Parmesan cheese, grated*

Peel potatoes and boil until done. Drain, then mash. Cool slightly; add egg and enough flour until it forms a soft dough. Make a roll about 1/2 inch in diameter. Cut into 1/2 inch pieces. Place on a board or tray to dry for 2 to 3 hours. Cook in boiling water to which a few drops of oil have been added. Cook until gnocchi sinks. Drain; place in bowl, spoon on desired sauce, mix gently. Serve with Parmesan cheese.

"This is one of our family's favorite dishes. They are quite filling so be careful not to overeat!"

Maria Fregulia   **Lassen Union High School, Susanville, CA**

ITALIAN SAUSAGE CRESCENT

Serves 4   ITALY

3/4 pound sweet Italian sausage,
*   ground beef or combination of both*
1/3 cup green pepper, chopped
3 tablespoons Ragu sauce
2 cups flour
1 tablespoon sugar
1 teaspoon salt
1/2 teaspoon Italian seasoning

1 package rapid rise yeast
1/2 cup hot water
2 tablespoons margarine, softened
2 eggs
3/4 cup mozzarella cheese, shredded
vegetable oil
1 teaspoon cold water
Parmesan cheese, grated

In large skillet, brown meat until lightly browned. Add green pepper and Ragu sauce and blend well. Remove from heat; drain well, set aside. Meanwhile, set aside 1/2 cup flour. In a large bowl, mix remaining flour, sugar, salt, Italian seasoning and yeast. Stir hot water and margarine into dry mixture. Mix in 1 egg and only enough reserved flour to make a soft dough. On lightly floured surface, knead until smooth and elastic, about 4 - 6 minutes. Roll dough to a 14" x 8" rectangle. Stir mozzarella cheese into meat mixture; spoon meat mixture down center of dough length. Bring long edges of dough together over filling; seal seam and ends. Shape into crescent and place seam side down on a greased baking sheet. Brush loaf with oil; cover loosely with plastic wrap. Refrigerate overnight or up to 24 hours. When ready to bake, remove from refrigerator. Uncover loaf carefully, making 4 slashes in top of each loaf. Let stand at room temperature for 10 minutes. Beat remaining egg with cold water and brush on loaf. Bake at 400 degrees for 25 minutes or until done. During last 2 minutes of baking, brush again with egg mixture; sprinkle with Parmesan cheese. Serve warm.

"This recipe came from Fleischman's Yeast Company. We make it in our foods lab, and the students really love it!"

Carleen Street   **Wasco Union High School, Wasco, CA**

BAGNA CAUDA

Serves a crowd   ITALY

1 1/2 quarts olive oil
1 pound butter

1 - 2 cups garlic, chopped
2 cans anchovies, chopped

<u>*Enough of the following for the number of people being served:*</u>
*mushrooms, sliced
*cabbage, sliced
*zucchini, sliced
*carrots, sliced
*brussel sprouts, halved

*cauliflower pieces
*artichoke hearts
*broccoli flowerets
*beef, venison or elk, cubed
*French rolls

Pour olive oil into a large frying pan or electric skillet. Add all butter as oil begins to warm. Add garlic and anchovies. Simmer for 1-1/2 hours. Stir often, watching carefully so mixture does not burn. Place enough meat and vegetables for 2 to 3 people into oil mixture. Fry several minutes until done. Remove with a slotted spoon to sliced halves of French rolls placed on dinner plates. Continue with remaining ingredients until everyone has been served.

"We usually have this between Christmas and New Years. It is excellent and it certainly helps if everyone eats it since it contains so much garlic!"

Maria Fregulia   **Lassen Union High School, Susanville, CA**

BEEROCKS (GERMAN MEAT TURNOVERS)

Serves 12   **GERMANY**

2 (1 pound) loaves frozen bread dough   *1 small head cabbage, chopped*
1 pound ground beef   *2 tablespoons worcestershire sauce*
1 medium onion, chopped   *2 teaspoons caraway seeds*
1 clove garlic, pressed   *butter or egg wash (1 egg white +*
1 1/2 teaspoon salt   *   2 tablespoons water), optional*
1 1/2 teaspoon lemon pepper

Let frozen bread dough thaw until pliable (use microwave if necessary). In a skillet, cook ground beef, onion, garlic, salt and lemon pepper until beef is browned. Add cabbage, worcestershire sauce and caraway seeds. Cook until cabbage is limp. Drain liquid from filling mixture. On a lightly floured board, roll each loaf of dough into a 12" circle. Cut each circle into 6 wedges. Spoon cabbage-meat filling onto center of each dough piece, dividing equally. Pull three points of each wedge up to the center and pinch to seal. Using a little flour on the fingers, pinch side edges to seal around filling making 3 seams. Place Beerocks on lightly greased cookie sheet. If desired, brush dough with melted butter or egg wash (1 egg white with 2 tablespoons water). Bake at 350 degrees for 30 minutes or until golden brown. Serve hot or wrap and freeze for heating later.

"This was given to me by my aunt. She would serve it during Oktoberfest."

Tricia Bergmann-Montelongo   **South Junior High School, Anaheim, CA**

CALZONES

Serves 6   **ITALY**

Crust:
2 1/2 - 3 cups flour   *1 cup warm water (115 - 120 degrees)*
1 package dry yeast   *2 tablespoons oil*
1/2 teaspoon salt   *2 tablespoons oil*

Filling:
1 pound ground meat, beef or pork   *3 tablespoons water*
1 cup onion, chopped   *1 1/2 cups mozzarella/cheese cheese,*
1/2 cup green pepper, chopped   *   shredded*
2 tomatoes, chopped   *1 egg, slightly beaten with 1 tablespoon*
1/3 cup tomato paste   *   water*
1 teaspoon basil, 1/2 teaspoon thyme,
*   1/2 teaspoon salt*

Crust: In a large bowl, combine 1 1/4 cups flour, yeast and salt. Add warm water and oil. Beat at low speed on electric mixer for 1/2 minute, scraping sides of bowl. Beat 3 minutes on high. Stir in remaining flour to form a dough; turn out on a floured board and knead 6 - 8 minutes. Cover and let rest 10 minutes. Divide into 6 parts and roll into 8 inch circles. Let rise for 20 minutes.

Filling: Cook ground meat with onion and green pepper until vegetables are tender. Drain. Combine tomatoes, tomato paste, seasonings and 3 tablespoons water. Add to meat mixture. Spoon onto crust circles. Sprinkle with cheese. Moisten edge of dough with mixture of egg and water. Fold in half. Seal edges. Prick tops. Brush with egg mixture. Bake on greased baking sheet and bake at 375 degrees for 25 to 30 minutes.

"You can add to or change filling to suit your family taste. A favorite of all my classes."

Sally Oxford   **Monache High School, Porterville, CA**

CORNISH PASTIES

Serves 6   **ENGLAND**

Pastry:
3 cups flour   *1 cup shortening*
1 teaspoon salt   *2/3 cup water*

Filling:
6 medium potatoes, peeled and   *1 pound lean pork steak, cut into*
*   sliced thin*   *   1/2 inch cubes*
1 pound round steak, cut into   *2 medium onions, sliced thin*
*   1/2 inch cubes*   *salt and pepper to taste*

Pastry: Combine flour and salt; cut in shortening until dough resembles small peas. Lightly stir in water and then divide dough into 6 parts. Roll each piece of dough in an oblong shape, 8" x 12".

Filling: On half of dough, layer potatoes, cubed meat, onion, and salt and pepper. Bring opposite end of pastry dough across top and crimp edges together to seal. Make 4 - 5 slits on the top. Bake at 375 degrees for 1 hour.

Jill Burnham   **Bloomington High School, Bloomington, CA**

ANTIPASTO "SANDWICHES"

Serves 2 - 5   **ITALY**

1 (6 - 7 ounce) can salmon   *1 jar marinated red peppers, drained*
1 Boboli bread   *Parmesan cheese*
1 (6 ounce) jar marinated artichoke
*   hearts, drained, reserving oil*

Drain salmon and spread over Boboli bread. Cut the artichokes into smaller pieces. Distribute artichokes and peppers over the boboli. Drizzle some of the reserved oil over the boboli. Sprinkle with freshly grated Parmesan cheese. Bake at 375 degrees for 10 to 12 minutes.

"Possible substitutions and/or additions include olives, additional artichokes, marinated onions and pimentos. ENJOY!!"

Kris Hawkins   **Clovis West High School, Fresno, CA**

GIANT BAKED ITALIAN CLUB SANDWICH

Serves 8 - 10   **ITALY**

2 (1 pound) loaves frozen bread dough
2 tablespoons dry Italian salad
dressing mix
4 tablespoons olive oil, divided
1 onion, thinly sliced
2 tablespoons red wine vinegar
1 clove garlic

1/2 pound mushroom, sliced
1 (6 ounce) jar marinated artichoke
hearts
1/2 pound turkey breast, sliced
1/2 pound ham, sliced
1/2 pound bacon, cooked
2 cups Swiss or jack cheese, shredded

Let dough thaw until pliable. Combine dressing mix with 2 tablespoons olive oil and set aside. Heat 1 tablespoon oil in medium skillet. Combine onion with wine vinegar, then pour into hot oil in skillet. Cook until onion is translucent. Drain thoroughly; pat dry and set aside. Heat 1 tablespoon oil and saute garlic and mushrooms; drain thoroughly; set aside. Drain artichoke hearts and slice; pat dry. Roll out dough on floured surface to 16" x 10" rectangle. Transfer to a greased baking sheet. Brush dough with salad dressing mixture. Cover half the dough lengthwise with layers of turkey, ham, bacon, onion, mushrooms, cheese and artichoke hearts. Fold plain half of dough over filling and seal edges together. Cut 3 small slits on top of sandwich to allow steam to escape. Brush dough with olive oil, then let rise in warm place about 30 minutes. Bake at 375 degrees until golden and sandwich sounds hollow when tapped, about 25 minutes. Cut into 2" slices.

Brenda Umbro   **Orange Glen High School, Escondido, CA**

FETTUCINI ALFREDO SAUCE

Serves 4   **ITALY**

3/4 to 1 cube butter, room temperature
2 cloves garlic, minced or pressed
2 tablespoons parsley, finely chopped
3 to 5 tablespoons Parmesan cheese,
grated

1/3 to 1/2 cup heavy cream
1/2 pound fettucini noodles, cooked
Optional: cooked chicken

Cook the fettucini noodles according to package directions. Using a food processor, put the butter in with the steel blade and process on and off quickly. Add garlic, parsley, Parmesan cheese and again process quickly on and off. Add cream, process on and off 1 to 2 times. Put sauce over warm noodles. You may add more cheese.

"Everyone likes this. You can have it as a meatless dinner or add chicken if you like."

Beverly Fincher-Ranger   **Carpinteria High School, Carpinteria, CA**

ITALIAN CLAM SAUCE

Serves 3   **ITALY**

2 tablespoons olive oil
2 tablespoons margarine
1 - 2 cloves garlic, minced
1 tablespoon flour
2 tablespoons Parmesan cheese
1 can minced clams, with juice to equal
   1 cup (add milk if necessary)

3/4 teaspoon dried basil
1/2 teaspoon oregano
dash of salt
dash of pepper
1 tablespoon dried parsley

Heat oil, margarine and garlic on low heat in a heavy saucepan. Stir the flour thoroughly into the melted fat until mixture is fairly smooth. Add Parmesan cheese and stir until blended. Remove pan from heat. Very slowly add the clams and liquid to the fat, cheese and flour mixture blending until it is fairly smooth. Add remaining seasonings. Return to heat and cook slowly, stirring constantly until sauce thickens and looks fairly smooth and glossy. Serve over cooked pasta.

"My thanks to Barsha Elzey, my high school Home Economics teacher, for this recipe. I prepared this recipe in her class years ago, and it has been a favorite ever since!"

Maria Montemagni   **Strathmore Union High School, Strathmore, CA**

MARINARA TOMATO SAUCE

Serves 4 - 5   **ITALY**

3 pounds ripe plum tomatoes or over ripe
   regular tomatoes
1/2 cup olive oil
2 carrots, finely chopped
2 celery stalks, finely chopped

1 medium onion, finely chopped
1/2 cup fresh basil, loosely packed
1/2 cup parsley, loosely packed
2 - 3 cloves garlic, minced
salt and freshly ground pepper to taste

Cut tomatoes into large pieces. Heat oil in a large saucepan. Add tomatoes, carrots, celery, onion, basil, parsley, garlic and salt and pepper. Bring to a boil. Reduce heat to medium. Cook, uncovered, 30 to 40 minutes until sauce reaches a medium-thick consistency. Taste and adjust for seasoning. Press everything through a food mill and back into saucepan. Cook 20 to 30 minutes longer.

"Makes 4 1/2 cups of sauce."

Diana F. Hill   **Sunnymead Middle School, Moreno Valley, CA**

SALSA PIZZAIOLA (TOMATO & GARLIC SAUCE)

Makes 3 cups   **ITALY**

3 tablespoons olive oil
1 cup onions, finely chopped
1 tablespoon garlic, finely chopped
4 cups Italian plum or whole canned
   tomatoes, undrained
1 (6 ounce) can tomato paste

1 tablespoon dried oregano
1 tablespoon fresh basil, chopped finely
1 bay leaf
2 teaspoons sugar
1 1/2 teaspoons salt
freshly ground pepper

In a 4 quart sauce pan, heat olive oil and cook onions over moderate heat for 7 to 8 minutes. When onions are transparent, NOT brown, add the garlic. Cook 1 to 2 minutes, stirring constantly. Stir in tomatoes and their liquid, tomato paste, oregano, basil, bay leaf, sugar, salt and pepper. Bring sauce to a boil, turn heat very low and simmer uncovered, stirring occasionally, for about 1 hour. When finished cooking, the sauce should be thick and fairly smooth. Remove the bay leaf. Taste and season the sauce with salt and freshly ground pepper. If you wish a smoother texture, puree the sauce through a food mill.

"This sauce may be served with spaghetti, ravioli and other pastas, or with meatballs. I have also added ground beef to the sauce and sweet or hot Italian sausage. I have used this sauce for pizza and lasagna. It keeps well in the freezer."

Beth Kolberg-Bentle **Rancho High School, North Las Vegas, NV**

SPAGHETTI SAUCE FOR A CROWD

Serves 50 - 75 **ITALY**

1 1/2 pounds boneless chuck roast
3/4 cup olive oil
1 1/2 cubes butter or margarine
6 onions, chopped
1 small carrot, finely chopped
2 ribs celery, finely chopped
1 head garlic, all cloves peeled and
*   minced*
1 bunch parsley, stemmed, cleaned
*   and minced*

1 cup dried mushrooms
2 (#10) cans whole tomatoes, pureed
1 (#10) can tomato sauce
2 tablespoons sugar
1/4 cup fresh thyme
2 tablespoons fresh marjoram
1 tablespoon leaf oregano
1 tablespoon sweet basil leaves
dash of cinnamon and cloves

In a large 3 gallon pot, brown meat in oil and butter until very dark on all sides and butter/ oil is very dark. Meanwhile chop all fresh vegetables. Remove meat from oil. Put all vegetables in oil with garlic and parsley. Saute until transparent. Cover mushrooms with water in a saucepan and simmer on stove. Add tomatoes to vegetables. Return meat to pot with vegetables, tomatoes and tomato sauce. Drain mushrooms, saving liquid and chop if needed; add to tomato mixture. Add sugar and seasonings. Bring sauce to boil and turn to low heat; simmer for at least 3 - 4 hours. Meat should break apart, if not, take out and shred, then return to pot. If sauce gets too thick, add reserved juice from mushrooms to thin.

"Mother's recipe - can be canned or frozen. Dried mushrooms make this recipe. I give it as Christmas presents."

Simon Clements **Bret Harte High School, Altaville, CA**

CHERRY OMELET

Serves 4 **GERMANY**

2 cups flour
1 cup milk
2 eggs
oil for frying

1 pound fresh Bing cherries, pitted
1/2 cup white sugar
1/4 teaspoon cinnamon

Mix together flour, milk and eggs; beat until smooth. Heat a heavy frypan, with lid, and add oil to coat the bottom of pan. Add 1/2 cup of the batter and sprinkle about 1/4 of the cherries on top of batter of each omelet. Cook over medium heat until the bottom of dough is light brown. Flip or turn the omelet over in pan with cherries under the dough. Put lid on pan and reduce heat. Cook until dough is done and cherries are tender. Slide onto plate and sprinkle with cinnamon/sugar mixture. Continue preparing remaining omelets.

"In my husband's family, this dish is eaten as a meal for lunch or light dinner. I learned the recipe from watching my German mother-in-law prepare it. It is of German origin and no known written recipe exists until now!"

Joyce Grohman   **Bellflower High School, Bellflower, CA**

FRITATTA ITALIANO OMELETTE

Serves 12   **ITALY**

8 ounces sweet Italian sausage   *salt and pepper to taste*
dash of olive oil   *4 ounces butter*
1 bell pepper, sliced   *24 eggs, beaten*
1 large onion, sliced   *4 ounces fresh Parmesan cheese,*
2 ounces fresh basil, chopped   *grated*

Place Italian sausage on a baking tray and bake at 350 degrees for 30 to 40 minutes, or until golden brown. Cool sausage and slice into bite-size pieces. In a saute pan, heat a dash of olive oil and add peppers and onions. Cook over medium heat until tender. Add sausage pieces and continue until thoroughly warmed. Add chopped basil and season to taste; set aside. In an omelette pan, heat butter and add eggs. (NOTE: a fritatta is served open faced and not folded like a French omelette). At this point, spoon in the sausage mixture and cook until firm on the bottom. Flip over and repeat on the reverse side. Grate the Parmesan cheese on top and serve.

"This is a great brunch for large or small groups. It makes a great Christmas breakfast."

Teena Sobey   **Chaparral High School, Las Vegas, NV**

CREPES LORRAINE

Serves 6   **FRANCE**

3 eggs, beaten   *1 cup mushrooms, sliced*
2/3 cups flour   *1/4 cup butter*
1/2 teaspoon salt   *3 tablespoons flour*
2 1/2 cups milk, divided   *2 chicken bouillon cubes*
1 package Swiss cheese slices, cut   *1/2 cup boiling water*
*   into strips*   *1/4 cup Parmesan cheese, grated*
2 cups ham, finely chopped   *1 tablespoon chives, chopped*
1 1/2 cups asparagus, cooked

Combine eggs, flour, salt and 1 cup milk; beat until smooth. Let batter set for 30 minutes before making crepes. If you have a "crepe maker iron", dip pan into batter, and remove from iron when cooked. If you're using a "crepe pan", place 2 to 3 tablespoons batter into pan and cook until crepe loosens from sides of pan. The darker side of finished crepe is the "presentation" side. Combine cheese, ham and asparagus; mix lightly. Fill each crepe with 2/3 cup ham mixture; roll up. Place crepes in a 9" x 13" baking dish and bake at 350 degrees for 30 minutes. Saute mushrooms in butter, blend in flour. Dissolve bouillon in boiling water and gradually add to mushroom mixture. Stir in remaining 1 1/2 cups milk and cook, stirring constantly until thickened. Add Parmesan cheese and chives; stir until cheese is melted. Serve sauce over crepes.

Judy Hevener   **Porterville High School, Porterville, CA**

STUFFED GRAPE LEAVES

Serves 8   GREECE

1 (9 ounce) jar grapevine leaves
4 medium onions, chopped
1 teaspoon salt
3 tabelspoons olive oil
1 1/2 pounds ground beef or lamb
2/3 cups rice, uncooked

1/4 teaspoon pepper
1 teaspoon fresh mint, snipped or
*   1/2 teaspoon dried mint flakes*
1 1/2 cups water
3 eggs
3 tablespoons lemon juice

Wash and drain grape leaves. Cook and stir onions and salt in oil until tender, about 5 minutes. Mix half the cooked onions, lamb, rice, pepper and mint. Place rounded measuring tablespoon of meat mixture on center of double layer of grape leaves. Fold stem ends over filling; fold in sides. Roll up tightly. Place seam side down in 12 inch skillet. Repeat with remaining meat mixture and leaves. Add water and remaining cooked onions. Beat eggs about 3 minutes. Slowly beat in lemon juice. Pour over grape leaves; bring to a boil, then lower heat and simmer 10 to 15 minutes.

Susan Keema   **Cimarron-Memorial High School, Las Vegas, NV**

SAUERKRAUT AND PORK ROAST WITH SPATZEN

Serves 6- 8   GERMANY

2 (28 ounce) cans sauerkraut, drained
1 (12 ounce) can beer

3 - 4 pounds pork roast
1/2 apple, sliced

Spatzen (Noodles):
2 cups all purpose flour
1/4 teaspoon salt

2 eggs
1/2 cup milk (approximate)

Place sauerkraut in roasting pan with beer, pork roast and apple. Bake at 325 degrees for 3 1/2 - 4 hours. Meanwhile, make spatzen. Mix together flour, salt and eggs. Add enough milk to make a thick paste. Bring a large pan of water to a boil. To cook spatzen, either run through a ricer or put batter on a plate and as it slides off the plate, cut off slices, forming "noodles". As you do this, the batter should be dropping into boiling water and cooked 2 to 3 minutes, until noodles are puffed. Serve spatzen with roast pork and sauerkraut.

"Old German recipe."

Theresa Campbell   **John F. Kennedy High School, La Palma, CA**

LASAGNA

Serves 8   ITALY

1 cup onions, chopped
1 pound ground beef
3 links hot sausage
3 cloves garlic, minced
2 teaspoons olive oil
1 tablespoon oregano OR Italian
    seasoning

1 teaspoon each salt and pepper
1 large can crushed tomatoes
1 (8 ounce) can tomato sauce
1/2 cup Parmesan cheese
1 pound mozzarella cheese, sliced
1 pound ricotta cheese
1 package lasagna noodles

Saute onion, beef, sausage and garlic in oil until brown. Mix all ingredients (except cheese and noodles) and simmer for 1 1/2 hours. In a 9" x 13" pan, layer: sauce, noodles, mozzarella, ricotta and Parmesan. Repeat. End with sauce and Parmesan cheese. Cook for 1 hour at 350 degrees.

"Well worth the time! I got this recipe many years ago from my sister, Lori. A family favorite - it also freezes well."

Cari Sheridan   **Grace Yokley Junior High School, Ontario, CA**

CHICKEN CACCIATORA

Serves 8 - 10   ITALY

3 pounds chicken breast halves
flour, for coating
2 tablespoons butter
2 tablespoons olive oil
2 cloves garlic, minced
2 medium onions, chopped
1 (1 pound 12 ounce) can Italian style
    tomatoes or stewed tomatoes
1 green pepper, sliced

2 tablespoons pimento, chopped
2 tablespoons parsley, chopped
1 teaspoon salt
1/2 teaspoon oregano, crumbled
1/2 teaspoon thyme, crumbled
1/4 teaspoon pepper
2/3 cup chicken broth
2 cups fresh mushrooms, thinly sliced

Rinse and dry chicken and cover lightly with flour. Melt butter and oil in a large frying pan and brown chicken on all sides. Remove from pan. Saute garlic and onion in pan until tender. Put chicken back into pan and add remaining ingredients EXCEPT mushrooms. Cover and simmer on medium heat 45 - 60 minutes until tender. Add mushrooms and cook 10 - 15 minutes longer. Remove chicken and vegetables to warm platter. Boil liquid until slightly reduced and thickened and pour over chicken. Garnish with parsley and serve over spaghetti.

"This is my family's favorite working together in the kitchen recipe. I make the chicken, Dad makes the green salad and Amber prepares the garlic bread!"

Donna Hamilton   **Del Oro High School, Loomis, CA**

CHICKEN MILANO

Serves 4   ITALY

2 cloves garlic, finely minced
4 half chicken breasts, boneless and
    skinless
1/2 teaspoon basil, crushed
1/8 teaspoon crushed red pepper flakes
    (optional)
1 tablespoon olive oil

1 (14 1/2 ounce) can Del Monte Italian
    Style Stewed Tomatoes
1 (16 ounce) can Del Monte Cut Green
    Italian Beans or Blue Lake Cut Green
    Italian Beans, drained
1/4 cup whipping cream

Rub garlic over chicken. Sprinkle with basil and red pepper. Season to taste with salt and pepper, if desired. In skillet, brown chicken in oil. Stir in tomatoes. Cover and simmer 5 minutes. Uncover and cook over medium heat, 8 to 10 minutes, or until liquid is slightly thickened. Stir in green beans and whipping cream; heat through. DO NOT BOIL.

Del Monte Foods   **San Francisco, CA**

FILETTO DI POLLO CON FUNGHI

Serves 4 - 5   ITALY

4 - 6 boneless, skinless chicken breasts
1/2 cup milk
1 egg
1 1/2 cups flour
1 clove garlic, minced
1/4 cup margarine or butter

2 cups mushrooms, sliced
1 cup green pepper, chopped
1/2 cup white onions, sliced
1 cup chicken broth (or bouillon)
1 cup white wine

Pound chicken breasts to tenderize. Combine milk and egg. Dredge chicken in this mixture; dredge in flour. Chill chicken for at least 1 hour. Saute garlic in small amount of butter. Brown chicken breast in garlic butter; remove from pan. Saute mushroom, green pepper and onions in same pan. Combine chicken broth and white wine in a small saucepan and simmer for 10 minutes. Put chicken back in pan with vegetables, pour wine mixture over and simmer another 10 to 15 minutes. Serve with rice or noodles.

"Translated, this recipe is Boneless Chicken Breast With Mushrooms. Serve with a crisp Caesar salad, sourdough bread and your favorite bottle of white wine."

Trena Becker   **Ball Junior High School, Anaheim, CA**

POLLO DEL SOL

Serves 4   ITALY

4 half chicken breasts
3 tablespoons olive oil
4 cloves garlic, minced
1 onion, finely chopped
3/4 cup dry white wine

salt and pepper, to taste
1 small lemon, thinly sliced, seeds
removed
4 sun-dried or oven-dried tomatoes
12 Italian dried olives

Wash chicken breasts and blot with paper towels until they are dry. Heat olive oil in a large skillet. When oil is very hot, but not smoking, saute the breasts skin-side down. Saute for 10 minutes on one side, then 5 minutes on other side. Remove from skillet and set aside. Using the same skillet, cook the garlic and onions over medium heat for 5 minutes, or until the onions are tender. Over high heat, add wine and chicken breasts. Add salt and pepper to taste, cover, and simmer for 15 minutes. After 15 minutes, turn chicken breasts over and add lemon slices, tomatoes and olives. Cover and cook 15 minutes more. Remove chicken from skillet and arrange on platter. Turn up heat and quickly reduce the liquid until it starts to become syrupy. Spoon the sauce over chicken breasts and serve.

"A very special chicken recipe - a favorite of our family!"

Helen Lievre   **La Canada High School, La Canada, CA**

HUHNERSCHNITZEL

Serves 4   **AUSTRIA**

1 pound boneless, skinless chicken
*   breast*
1 cup bread crumbs
1 teaspoon seasoned salt
2 tablespoons Parmesan cheese

1/4 teaspoon paprika
1 egg, beaten with 2 tablespoons
*   water*
butter and oil for frying

Pound chicken breasts. Combine bread crumbs, seasoned salt, Parmesan cheese and paprika. Dip chicken pieces first in flour, then in egg, and finally in the bread crumb mixture. Place the breaded chicken pieces in the refrigerator for one half hour to one hour. Heat a mixture of butter and oil, 1/4 inch deep in a skillet. Cook chicken about 5 minutes on each side, until golden brown. Place on a paper towel-lined plate when done.

"This dish is my children's favorite. In fact, they just refer to it as our Favorite Chicken"

Katherine Iverson   **Vandenberg Middle School, Lompoc, CA**

CHICKEN CACCIATORE

Serves 4 - 6   **ITALY**

2 cloves garlic, finely minced
1/2 cup olive oil
2 - 3 pounds frying chicken pieces
1/2 cup flour
2 3/4 teaspoons salt
3/4 teaspoon pepper
1/2 teaspoon Accent

3 tablespoons shortening
2 tablespoons butter
1 small onion, sliced
2 small can mushrooms
1 (12-1/2 ounce) canned tomatoes, sieved
1 teaspoon oregano
1 teaspoon parsley, chopped

Heat the garlic in olive oil; set aside. Shake chicken in a bag with flour, 1 1/2 teaspoons of the salt, 1/4 teaspoon of the pepper and Accent. Heat shortening and place chicken skin-side down to brown. While chicken is browning, heat butter in a small skillet. Add onion and mushrooms. Saute slowly until onion is transparent and mushrooms are slightly browned. Add this mixture to the chicken with sieved tomatoes, remaining salt and pepper, oregano, parsley and garlic. Cook 25 to 30 minutes until chicken is tender. If mixture thickens, a little water can be added.

"Another delicious recipe from Grandma!! Serve with favorite pasta."
Judy Tomlinson   **Colusa High School, Colusa, CA**

GREEK STYLE HAMBURGERS

Serves 4 - 6   **GREECE**

1 1/4 pounds ground beef
1/2 teaspoon salt
1/4 teaspoon pepper
1/4 teaspoon thyme
1/4 cup parsley, chopped
2 tablespoons fresh celery leaves,
    chopped
1 medium onion, chopped

1/2 cup cooked rice
3 tablespoons butter
3 tablespoons tomato paste
1 1/2 tablespoons flour
1/2 cup beef broth
1/4 cup red wine
1/4 cup sour cream

Combine meat, spices, celery leaves, onion and rice with hands. Shape into 2 inch diameter patties and brown in melted butter. Remove patties from pan. To the drippings, add tomato paste and flour. Add broth and wine and cook until thickened. Add a little water if necessary. Add sour cream to sauce and return patties to pan. Spoon sauce over patties and simmer 10 minutes.

"I usually double the amount of sauce."

Janet Riness   **Westminster High School, Westminster, CA**

VEAL PARMIGIANA

Serves 4 - 5   **ITALY**

1/2 pound veal, cut 1/4" thick
1/2 cup + 2 tablespoons fine dry
    bread crumbs
1/4 cup Parmesan cheese, grated
1 egg, well beaten
2 teaspoons water

1/2 teaspoon salt
1/8 teaspoon pepper
1/3 cup oil
8 ounces of your favorite pasta sauce
5 slices mozzarella cheese

Cut veal into 5 pieces; pound with mallet to tenderize. Combine bread crumbs and Parmesan cheese; set aside. Mix together egg, water, salt and pepper. Heat oil to 350 degrees in an electric skillet. Dip cutlets into egg mixture and then in bread crumbs. Brown in skillet. Pour sauce over veal. Top with mozzarella cheese. Turn skillet down to simmer and cook gently until cheese is melted.

"Not difficult and very tasty!"
Gloria Reece   **Porterville High School, Porterville, CA**

GLAZED CORNED BEEF BRISKET

Serves 6   IRELAND

4 to 5 pound piece of corned beef   *1/4 cup vinegar*
1 tablespoon prepared mustard   *1/4 cup pineapple juice*
1/3 cup brown sugar   *2 tablespoons butter*
1/3 cup catsup

Place meat in large kettle; cover with cold water and bring to a boil. Skim off any solids which rise to the surface in the first 5 to 10 minutes of cooking. Cover pan and reduce heat. Simmer 3 to 3 1/2 hours. Remove meat from liquid and place on rack in a shallow pan. Combine mustard, brown sugar, catsup, vinegar and pineapple juice and butter in a saucepan. Bring to a boil stirring constantly for 2 minutes. Pour sauce over brisket and bake at 350 degrees for 25 to 30 minutes. Spoon sauce over meat frequently.

"A little extra work but worth it. Cabbage and carrots and potatoes can be cooked in the liquid while corned beef is in the oven."

Linda Hsieh   **Rowland High School, Rowland Heights, CA**

PASTITSIO

Serves 15 - 20   GREECE

Part 1
1 pound ground chuck   *1/2 teaspoon salt*
1 tablespoon butter   *1/4 teaspoon pepper*
1/2 medium onion, grated   *1 1/2 tablespoons tomato paste*
1/4 teaspoon cinnamon   *1/4 cup water*

Part 2
1/2 cup butter   *3 cups mlk*
3/4 cup flour

Part 3
1 quart water   *1/2 cup butter*
1/2 teaspoon salt   *1/2 cup Kefaloteri cheese, grated*
3/4 pound macaroni, medium size   *(or Romano)*

Part 4
3 egg yolks   *2 whole eggs*

Part 1: brown ground chuck in butter. Add remaining ingredients and simmer for 20 minutes; set aside.

Part 2: Melt butter in saucepan. Add flour and blend, using a wooden spoon. Slowly add milk, stirring constantly and rapidly, until thick and smooth. Set aside to cool.

Part 3: Bring water and salt to a boil in large saucepan. Add macaroni and boil for 8 - 10 minutes, until done. Drain, rinse under running hot water. Drain thoroughly. Melt butter in pan and add macaroni and cheese; mix well.

Part 4: Beat eggs until fluffy. Add to white sauce in Part 2. Mix thoroughly.

Part 5: Add 1/2 or less of white sauce to macaroni mixture. Pour half of this into a greased baking pan (17" x 11" x 2); top with meat mixture, spreading evenly over entire surface. Pour remaining macaroni over meat, spread evenly. Top with remaining white sauce. Spread evenly and bake at 375 degrees for 30 minutes, or until lightly browned on to When slightly cooled, cut into squares for 15 to 20 generous servings.

"This may be made the day before and reheated. Also may be frozen."

Janet Griffith   **Norco High School, Norco, CA**

TOMATO PESTO LASAGNA

Serves 6   **ITALY**

8 ounces lasagna noodles	3/4 cup water
1 pound sausage or ground beef, crumbled	8 ounces ricotta cheese
1 (14 1/2 ounce) can Del Monte Pasta Style Chunky Tomatoes	1 (4 ounce) package frozen pesto, thawed*
	2 cups mozzarella cheese, shredded
1 (6 ounce) can Del Monte Tomato Paste	

Cook noodles according to package directions; rinse, drain and separate noodles. In a large skillet, brown meat; drain. Stir in tomatoes, tomato paste and water; mix well. In a 2 quart or 9" square baking dish, layer 1/3 meat sauce, half of the noodles, ricotta, pesto and mozzarella cheese; repeat layers ending with sauce. Top with Parmesan cheese, if desired. Bake at 350 degrees for 30 minutes or until heated through.

*Helpful hint: pesto is available frozen or refrigerated at the supermarket.

Del Monte Foods   **San Francisco, CA**

LASAGNA

Serves 12 - 16   **ITALY**

2 medium onions, chopped	1 (6 ounce) can tomato paste
1 - 2 green peppers, chopped	2 (6 ounce) cans tomatoes, pureed in blender
2 - 3 stalks celery, chopped	
1 - 2 cloves garlic, minced	1 teaspoon worcestershire sauce
1 - 1/2 pounds lean ground beef	1 pound Monterey jack cheese, shredded
1 pound Italian sausage	
salt and pepper, to taste	1 pound mozzarella cheese, shredded
1 teaspoon oregano	1 pound lasagna noodles
1/4 cup wine vinegar	Parmesan cheese, to taste
2 (8 ounce) cans tomato sauce	

Saute onions, peppers, celery and garlic in a small amount of oil until they turn yellow. Transfer to a large saucepot. Brown ground beef and Italian sausage, adding salt and pepper to taste. Add meats to the vegetables in saucepot. Add the oregano, wine vinegar, tomato sauce, tomato paste, tomatoes and worcestershire sauce; simmer the sauce for 1 hour. If the sauce seems thick, you may want to add another can of tomatoes or tomato sauce. Combine jack cheese and mozzarella cheese; set aside. Cook the lasagna noodles as directed on package. When ready to assemble the lasagna, using a deep 9" x 13" x 2 1/2" pan, put a layer of sauce, noodles, sauce and shredded cheese and continue layering ending with sauce on top. Sprinkle with Parmesan cheese, to taste. Bake at 350 degrees for 1 hour. Allow to set 10 to 15 minutes after removing from oven for easier serving.

"This is one of my favorite recipes! It is a good recipe for anyone who does not care for ricotta or cottage cheese which is in most lasagna recipes. Most of my students have tried this recipe."

Doris Oitzman   **Victor Valley High School, Victorville, CA**

ITALIAN STRATA

Serves 8 - 10   **ITALY**

8 slices bread
1 (8 ounce) ball mozzarella cheese,
*   shredded*
2 (14 1/2 ounce) can sliced tomatoes,
*   drained*
1 (30 ounce) can mushrooms, drained
1 medium onion, thinly sliced in rings

5 eggs
3 cups milk
1 1/2 teaspoons salt
1/2 teaspoon oregano
1/8 tablespoon garlic salt
Parmesan cheese

From bread, cut 8 donuts and holes, set aside. Fit scraps of bread in bottom of 13" x 9" x 2" greased pan. Top with a layer of cheese. Arrange tomato slices on top of cheese (reserving 8 slices for top). Layer mushrooms and onion rings over cheese. Add another layer of cheese. Arrange donuts and holes and tomato slices on top of cheese. Combine slightly beaten eggs, milk, salt, oregano and garlic; pour over bread. Sprinkle with Parmesan cheese. Cover with waxed paper and refrigerate overnight. Remove from refrigerator 1 hour before baking. Bake at 350 degrees for 1 to 1 1/2 hours. Insert a knife in center to determine doneness. Let stand 5 minutes before cutting.

"Make this dish ahead of time and refrigerate overnight. Bake in the morning."

Sheryl Holtz   **Redwood Intermediate School, Thousand Oaks, CA**

ITALIAN DISH

Serves 4   **ITALY**

2 cups macaroni shells, uncooked
3 tablespoons olive oil
1 pound ground beef
1 - 2 cloves garlic, minced
2 - 3 tablespoons parsley, chopped

1/2 teaspoon salt
1/4 teaspoon pepper
1 teaspoon whole leaf sage, crumbled
1 (8 ounce) can tomato sauce
Parmesan cheese

Cook macaroni shells according to package directions until tender but still chewy (al dente). Heat oil in fry pan; add ground beef and garlic and cook until browned. Add parsley, salt, pepper, sage and tomato sauce. Mix. Simmer on low for 15 to 20 minutes. Place macaroni shells on platter; spoon meat sauce on top and sprinkle with Parmesan cheese. Serve.

"This is an old family recipe. Very easy and very good."

Nancy Brunson   **McKinleyville High School, McKinleyville, CA**

CHEESE & RICE CASSEROLE

Serves 8   **ITALY**

2 cups water	*1 medium onion, chopped*
1 cup regular rice, uncooked	*1 medium green pepper, chopped*
1 teaspoon salt	*2 cups mozzarella or cheddar cheese*
1/2 teaspoon dry mustard	*4 eggs, slightly beaten*
1/2 teaspoon red pepper sauce	*2 1/2 cups milk*
1/4 teaspoon pepper	*1/2 cup Parmesan cheese, grated*

Heat water, rice, salt, mustard, red pepper sauce and pepper to boiling, stirring once or twice; reduce heat; cover and simmer 15 minutes (do not lift lid or stir). Remove from heat. Fluff rice lightly with fork; cover and let steam 10 minutes. In a 11" x 7" x 1 1/2" greased baking dish, layer 1/2 of the rice, onion, green pepper and cheese; repeat. Mix eggs and milk; pour over rice mixture. Sprinkle with Parmesan cheese. (Casserole can be covered and refrigerated up to 24 hours at this point.) Cook, uncovered, at 325 degrees for 45 to 50 minutes, until set. Let stand 10 minutes. Cut into squares.

"In Italian, this dish is Riso e Formaggio. The much praised rice of northern Italy (often found in American gourmet shops in small canvas bags at premium prices) is shorter and thicker than most American rice, and was so admired by Thomas Jefferson that he smuggled grains of it out of northern Italy in the eighteenth century and planted it in American soil!"

Colleen Easton   **Brea-Olinda High School, Brea, CA**

SPANISH MEAT LOAF

Serves 6   **SPAIN**

1 1/2 pounds ground beef	*1 egg*
1 (8 ounce) can tomato sauce	*1 teaspoon salt*
10 pimento-stuffed olives, sliced	*1/4 teaspoon pepper*
1/2 cup onion, chopped	*1 tablespoon worcestershire sauce*
1/3 cup oats	

Mix beef with 1/3 cup tomato sauce and the next six ingredients. Shape in an ungreased loaf pan. Mix remaining tomato sauce with worcestershire sauce and spread on top. Bake at 350 degrees for 1 hour + 15 minutes.

"I often make 2 or 3 of these at a time. I bake one and freeze the others for another time."

Alice Demele   **Colton High School, Colton, CA**

CHICKEN ROZ

Serves 4

1 medium eggplant
salt
2 eggs
2 tablespoons milk
4 cups fresh bread crumbs
olive oil
4 chicken breast halves

salt and pepper, to taste
1/4 cup flour
*fresh marinara sauce, recipe
    follows
2 tablespoons basil
1 (6 ounce) package mozzarella
    cheese, sliced

Slice eggplant 3/8 inch thick. Sprinkle with salt and let stand 30 minutes. Pat eggplant slices dry with paper towels. Beat eggs with milk. Dip eggplant slices in mixture, then bread crumbs. Reserve remaining egg mixture and crumbs for chicken. Place eggplant slices on lightly oiled jellyroll pans. Bake at 400 degrees 25 to 30 minutes or until browned and tender. Skin and bone chicken breast halves. Pound to flatten slightly, then sprinkle with salt and pepper. Dredge chicken with flour; dip in egg/milk mixture, then bread crumbs. Saute in olive oil until browned on both sides. Line 13" x 9" baking dish with eggplant slices. Top with 2 1/2 cups fresh marinara sauce. Add layer of chicken, then layer of eggplant slices. Pour remaining 2 1/2 cups fresh marinara sauce over top. Sprinkle with 1 tablespoon basil, then mozzarella slices in single layer over all. Bake at 350 degrees 20 to 30 minutes, until heated through and cheese has melted. Sprinkle with remaining 1 tablespoon basil.

"This is an excellent company meal!"

Libby Bruce   **Troy High School, Fullerton, CA**

FRESH MARINARA SAUCE

Makes 5 cups

2 cups onions, finely chopped
2 cloves garlic, minced
1/4 cup olive oil
8 large tomatoes

1/2 teaspoons crushed dried oregano
salt, to taste
pepper, to taste
2 tablespoons butter

Saute onions and garlic in olive oil until soft. Peel, seed and chop tomatoes. Add tomatoes, onions and garlic along with oregano. Cook 15 to 20 minutes, until slightly thick. Season to taste with salt and pepper. Swirl in butter.

Libby Bruce   **Troy High School, Fullerton, CA**

LASAGNA

Serves 15

1/2 pound ground beef
3/4 pound Italian sausage
1 large onion, chopped
3 cloves garlic, chopped
2 tablespoons ground oregano
1 (8 ounce) can tomato sauce
1 (6 ounce) can tomato paste

1 (28 ounce) can peeled tomatoes
salt and pepper, to taste
1 (16 ounce) ball mozzarella cheese
1 (8 ounce) carton ricotta cheese
lasagna noodles
1 (12 ounce) can tomato juice
Parmesan cheese

Brown meats and onion; drain off fat. Add garlic, oregano, tomato sauce, tomato paste and whole tomatoes. Salt and pepper to taste. Simmer 1 hour. Combine mozzarella cheese and ricotta cheese. Layer in large 10"x15" pan, 1/3 sauce, 1/3 cheese and a layer of uncooked noodles. Repeat 2 more times. Pour tomato juice on top and sprinkle with Parmesan cheese. Bake at 375° for 35-45 minutes. Let stand 5 minutes before serving.

"It takes a little longer to make the sauce from scratch, but it is well worth it. This recipe also freezes well, so eat half now and freeze half for later."

Cindy Bowman   **McFarland High School, McFarland, CA**

NONNIE'S FAMOUS SPAGHETTI

Serves 8   **ITALY**

2 pound top sirloin or round steak, cubes or cut into strips
1/2 small onion, chopped
4 ounces button mushrooms
1 (28 ounce) can whole tomatoes
1 (6 ounce) can black olives

1 (6 ounce) can tomato paste
1/4 clove garlic, minced
1 pound spaghetti
1/2 cube butter
2 pounds tillamook cheese

Brown meat and onion. Mix together mushrooms, tomatoes, olives, tomato paste and garlic; add to meat mixture. Cook spaghetti al dente. Mix cooked spaghetti, butter and tomato/meat mixture. Grate cheese into mixture but save some for top of casserole. Place mixture into a buttered casserole dish, adding a little water if necessary. Be sure olives are covered by cheese to avoid burning. Bake at 350 degrees for 1 hour.

"This is one of my family's favorite recipes and is much better on the second day!"

Lera St. Louis   **Buena High School, Ventura, CA**

FETTUCCINI ALFREDO A LA THOMAS

Serves 4   **ITALY**

1/3 cup onion, minced
2 - 4 cloves garlic, minced
1 habañero or 2 jalapeño chiles, minced
8 tablespoons butter, divided
1/2 cup white wine
1 cup heavy whipping cream
4 ounces Parmesan cheese, grated

1/2 teaspoon nutmeg
pepper, to taste
1/2 cup sour cream
1 pound fresh fettuccini pasta
1/2 pound medium shrimp, shelled and deveined
Parmesan cheese, for topping

Saute onion, garlic and chiles in 3 tablespoons butter; add wine, simmer and reduce until almost all liquid is gone; add 3 more tablespoons butter and melt. Over low heat, stir in cream, Parmesan cheese, nutmeg and pepper; when ingredients are blended, stir in sour cream until all ingredients are thoroughly blended. Turn off heat. In a large pot, bring water to a boil and cook fresh fettucini pasta. While pasta is cooking, saute shrimp in remaining 2 tablespoons butter . When pasta is done, drain thoroughly in colander. Pour alfredo sauce into pot and add pasta; drain any liquid from shrimp and add to pasta and sauce. Mix together gently to coat pasta and heat through.

"If you don't like spice, you can cut recipe with additional sour cream or leave out the chilies. If you like spice, don't use any sour cream."

Dale Thomas   **Mira Mesa High School, San Diego, CA**

SHELLFISH FETTUCCINI

Serves 4   ITALY

1 pound fettuccini, cooked and
    drained
1/2 cup butter
1/2 cup olive oil
1 cup dry white wine
6 large cloves garlic, minced
1 teaspoon crushed rosemary

2 cans clams, chopped
1 can baby shrimp
1 large tomato, peeled, seeded
    & chopped
1/2 teaspoon parsley
1/2 teaspoon sugar
salt & pepper to taste

In large skillet, heat butter and olive oil over moderate-high heat until mixture is bubbly.
Add wine, garlic and rosemary. cooking until wine is evaporated and butter is golden.
Reduce heat. Add clams and shrimp with their liquid. Add tomato, parsley, sugar, salt and
pepper. Cook until completely heated. Spoon over cooked fettuccini.

Barbara Gauthier   **Santana High School, Santee, CA**

LINGUINE WITH BOSCAIOLA SAUCE

Serves 4   ITALY

1/2 pound bacon, cut in pieces
1/2 pound mushrooms, sliced
3 cloves garlic, minced
1 1/2 teaspoons crushed red peppers
1/2 teaspoon salt
1/2 teaspoon basil

1 (1 pound) can tomatoes, peeled
    & chopped
1 pound linguine
1/2 cup olive oil
Romano cheese

Fry bacon, drain and set aside. Saute mushrooms, garlic and red pepper in small amount
of bacon drippings. Drain off fat. Add bacon to mushroom mixture, stir in salt, basil and
tomatoes. Simmer 5 minutes. Cook pasta in 3 quarts of rapidly boiling salted water until
al'dente. Drain. Toss with olive oil. Place in large soup bowls, top with sauce and serve with
Romano cheese.

"A good busy-day dinner!"

Pat Curtis   **Ensign Junior High School, Newport Beach, CA**

CHICKEN WITH SUN DRIED TOMATOES

Serves 4   ITALY

4 chicken breasts, cut into bite-sized
    pieces
2 tablespoons butter
1 1/2 cups mushrooms
1 - 2 cloves garlic, minced
1/3 cup sun-dried tomatoes, chopped

1/2 teaspoons crushed red pepper
1 cup heavy cream
1 cup chicken broth
1 package angel hair pasta
1/3 cup green onion, chopped
1/3 cup cilantro, chopped

Saute chicken breast pieces in butter. Add whole mushrooms, garlic, tomatoes and red pepper. Saute for an additional 3 minutes. Add cream and chicken broth; cook for 5 to 7 minutes. Prepare angel hair pasta according to package directions. Add green onions and cilantro to chicken mixture. Pour chicken mixture over pasta and serve.

Cari Barnard   **Murrieta Valley High School, Murrieta, CA**

NOODLE KUGEL

Serves 4 - 6   **EUROPE**

1 (10 ounce) package noodles   *3 tablespoons brown sugar*
2 eggs   *raisins (optional)*
1 cup sour cream   *cinnamon*
1 cup cottage cheese   *butter or margarine*

Cook noodles as package directs. Beat eggs and mix with sour cream, cottage cheese, brown sugar and raisins. Add drained noodles. Put into greased baking dish. Sprinkle with cinnamon and dot with butter. Bake at 350 degrees for 45 minutes.

Laurie Lucero   **Santa Maria High School, Santa Maria, CA**

PASTA FOUR FORMAGGI

Serves 6   **ITALY**

1 pound pasta of your choice   *1/2 cup Parmesan cheese, freshly*
3/4 cup light cream   *   grated*
1/3 cup Swiss cheese, grated   *salt, to taste*
1/3 cup gouda or edam cheese, grated *pepper, freshly ground, to taste*
1/4 cup Fontina cheese, slivered or   *1/2 cup Parmesan cheese, grated*
*   1/2 cup mozzarella, grated*   *   (for topping)*

Cook pasta in boiling, salted water until desired doneness; while cooking, prepare sauce. Pour light cream into another large saucepan. Add all the grated cheese, a little at a time. Simmer over very low heat, until cheese is completely melted. When the mixture is smooth, if needed, add salt and pepper to taste. Drain pasta and rinse quickly under cold water. Pour pasta, all at once, into the saucepan with the cheese. Toss quickly until all pasta is well coated. Place in a serving bowl and sprinkle with remaining Parmesan cheese.

"I first enjoyed this at a trattoria in Florence, Italy in 1979; later at Gianni's in Crystal Court in Costa Mesa, California. At home, I use variations of this to come close to memories of Florence."

Willy Hall   **Orange High School, Orange, CA**

PASTA E FAGIOLI (MACARONI & BEANS)

Serves 4 - 6   ITALY

1 medium onion, chopped
1 tablespoon oil
1 teaspoon olive oil
3 cloves garlic, peeled and sliced
5 (8 ounce) cans tomato sauce
4 (15 ounce) cans Great Northern
    beans, drained

10 leaves fresh basil, chopped
1 bay leaf
2 teaspoons salt
2 tablespoons oregano
2 1/2 cups elbow macaroni
Parmesan cheese

Fry onion in large pot with oils. Add garlic and fry 10 minutes. Add tomato sauce, drained beans and 1 1/2 cans (from beans) of water to pot; mix well. Add fresh basil, bay leaf, salt and oregano. Let simmer 1 1/2 to 2 hours, stirring often. During the last 1/2 hour, you may want to crush beans to cook down to a paste. In a separate pot, boil macaroni until done; drain, then combine with sauce and serve with Parmesan cheese.

"This authentic Italian recipe originates from my husband's Nana, a native of Sicily. It is known as a poor man's supper. It is a family favorite that is loved by all who try it."

Katie Placido   **Warren High School, Downey, CA**

LASAGNA

Serves 10 - 12   ITALY

1 1/2 pounds hamburger
2 (8 ounce) cans tomato sauce
1 can water
1 package Lawry's spaghetti sauce
    seasoning

11 lasagna noodles
1 small container Parmesan cheese
1 pound jack cheese, grated
1 pound mozzarella cheese, grated
1 (8 ounce) container cottage cheese

Brown hamburger; drain well. Add tomato sauce, water and seasoning mix. Cook for about 45 minutes to 1 hour. Cook lasagna noodles; boil about 15 to 20 minutes. Rub oil on bottom of large casserole dish. Put one layer of noodles, one layer of sauce, sprinkle with Parmesan, jack cheese, mozzarella cheese and cottage cheese. Repeat for 2nd layer. 3rd layer should be noodles, sauce and Parmesan cheese only. Bake 30 minutes at 350 degrees.

"Can be made ahead and refrigerated or frozen."

Rita Blohm   **Nogales High School, La Puente, CA**

STUFFED MANICOTTI

Serves 6   ITALY

Meat sauce:

1 garlic clove, crushed	1 can chopped tomatoes
1/2 cup onion, chopped	1 cup mushrooms, sliced
1 teaspoon margarine, melted	1 1/2 teaspoons salt
1/2 pound ground beef	1/2 teaspoon pepper
1/2 pound Italian sausage	1 tablespoon sugar
1 teaspoon flour	1 teaspoon crushed oregano
1 (29 ounce) can tomato sauce	3/4 teaspoon Italian seasoning

Cheese filling:

15 ounces ricotta cheese	1/2 cup Parmesan, grated
1 cup mozzarella, grated	1 egg, beaten

12 to 14 manicotti shells

Prepare meat sauce by sauteing crushed garlic and onion in melted margarine. Add ground beef and sausage and brown, breaking up meats. Drain off grease. Stir in flour, tomato sauce, canned tomatoes, mushrooms and all seasonings. Simmer, uncovered, for 15 minutes. Stir occasionally. Combine ingredients for cheese filling. Stuff, uncooked, manicotti shells with cheese filling. Cover bottom of baking pan with meat sauce. Arrange stuffed shells on top. Cover shells completely with remaining sauce. Cover with foil and bake at 375 degrees for 40 to 45 minutes.

Diana Lee   **Elsinore Middle School, Lake Elsinore, CA**

MANICOTTI W/MEAT OR CHEESE FILLING

Serves 4 - 6   ITALY

Spaghetti sauce:

1/4 pound lean hamburger	3 (8 ounce) cans tomato sauce
1/4 pound ground turkey	2 tablespoons Italian seasoning
1/2 small onion, minced	1/2 teaspoon dried oregano leaves
2 cloves garlic, minced	2 (8 ounce) cans water

Meat filling:

1/4 pound ground turkey	2 cloves garlic, minced
1/4 pound lean ground beef	1 cup spinach, thawed and drained
1/4 cup onion, minced	1 cup bread crumbs
1/2 teaspoon salt	1 egg, slightly beaten
1/8 teaspoon pepper	1/4 cup Parmesan cheese

Cheese filling:

2 cups ricotta cheese	2 tablespoons parsley, minced
1/4 cup Parmesan cheese, grated	1/4 teaspoon salt
1/8 teaspoon pepper	1 cup mozzarella, grated
1 package manicotti noodles	

Prepare sauce: brown hamburger, turkey, onion and garlic. Add tomato sauce, spices and water. Simmer for about 1 hour, adding water as needed. Meanwhile, prepare meat or cheese filling:

Meat Filling: brown and separate meat into small pieces. Pour off fat and add onion, salt, pepper and garlic. Remove from heat. Add spinach and remaining ingredients. Mix well and set aside.

Cheese Filling: Place all ingredients in a bowl and stir well. Set aside.

Prepare manicotti noodles according to package instructions. Drain. Place 1 cup spaghetti sauce on bottom of 13" x 9" pan. Fill manicotti noodles with desired filling and arrange in a single layer over sauce. Sprinkle with Parmesan cheese and spread with more sauce. Cover with foil and bake at 350 degrees for 20 minutes. Uncover and bake 10 minutes longer.

Rosemary A. Ross　　　　　　　**North High School, Bakersfield, CA**

SPINACH & CHEESE STUFFED MANICOTTI

Serves 4 - 6　　　　　　　　　　　　　　　　　　　　　　　**ITALY**

1 package manicotti
2 (9 ounce) packages frozen creamed
　spinach
1 (15 ounce) cartons ricotta cheese
1 (8 ounce) ball mozzarella cheese,
　grated

1 teaspoon salt
1/4 teaspoon pepper
1 pound ground beef
1 (32 ounce) jar spaghetti sauce

Cook manicotti as directed. Drain. Slit 1 side open. Cook creamed spinach according to package directions. Mix spinach with cheese, salt and pepper. Stuff manicotti shells. Place in a casserole dish. Cook ground beef and drain. Add to spaghetti sauce and pour over manicotti. Bake at 350 degrees for 40 minutes.

"To my most wonderful neighbor, Susie Portz, thank you for another fantastic recipe. I'm so lucky to have such a great cook living next door!!!"

Cheryl McDaniels　　　　　**Green Valley High School, Henderson, NV**

GREEK RICE PUDDING

Serves 6　　　　　　　　　　　　　　　　　　　　　　　**GREECE**

1/3 cup rice
1/8 teaspoon salt
1/3 cup water
1 quart milk, scalded
3/4 cup sugar

2 eggs
1/4 cup butter
1 teaspoon vanilla
cinnamon, for sprinkling on top

Cook rice in salted boiling water until water is absorbed; add hot milk and cook slowly until rice is tender. Add sugar and heat until sugar is dissolved. Remove pan from heat. In a bowl, beat eggs and stir a little of the hot milk mixture in them; add butter and stir until melted and blended. Pour this into the rice mixture. Return pan to stove and heat until creamy. Add vanilla; mix and pour into dessert dishes and sprinkle with cinnamon.

"A family favorite for more than 50 years."

Joanne Fial   **East Middle School, Downey, CA**

ICKY STICKY PUDDING

Serves 12 - 16   **ENGLAND**

12 ounces fresh dates, chopped   *12 ounces light brown sugar*
2 teaspoons soda   *4 eggs, beaten*
15 ounces water   *12 ounces self-rising flour*
4 1/2 ounces butter   *1 teaspoon vanilla*

Toffee sauce:
14 ounces light brown sugar   *8 ounces butter*
7 fluid ounces whipping cream   *1/2 teaspoon vanilla*

Preheat oven to 300 degrees. Place dates and soda in a pan with 15 ounces water and bring to a boil. Remove from heat and cool completely. Add butter, brown sugar, eggs, flour and vanilla to date mixture; beati until thoroughly mixed. Pour into greased pan and bake 1 hour. Make the sauce by putting all topping ingredients in saucepan and cooking until thickened and golden, stirring occasionally. Pour sauce over baked pudding and serve.

Pat Jones   **Buena High School, Ventura, CA**

GREEK BAKLAVA

Serves 20   **GREECE**

1 box phyllo dough (about 30 sheets,   *1 cup unsalted butter, clarified*
12" x 17") Apollo brand   *(2 sticks)*

Filling:
1 pound walnuts, finely ground   *1/2 cup granulated sugar*
(1/2 almonds may be used)   *1/4 teaspoon ground cinnamon*

Syrup:
2 cups granulated sugar   *2 teaspoons almond extract (or 1*
2 cups water   *tablespoon rose water)*
1 lemon peel strip (1/2" x 3") without
white membrane

Mix all the filling ingredients together and set aside in a bowl. Make syrup by bringing all ingredients, EXCEPT almond extract, to a boil in a saucepan. Simmer for 45 minutes, stirring occasionally. Remove from heat and lift out lemon peel strip. When cool, stir in almond extract. This syrup will be poured over the Baklava AFTER it has been baked.

Clarify unsalted butter by melting it over LOW heat until it bubbles and the sediment and water settle out to the bottom of the pan.

Open the box of phyllo and unwrap it into a stack of full sheets. Cut it in half to produce one stack of sheets that measure approximately 12" x 8" so it will fit into a 9" x 13" baking pan. Metal is preferred, but if glass is used, be sure to REDUCE the heat for baking to 300 degrees. To prevent phyllo sheets from drying out while working with them, place a damp towel on the counter with a sheet of waxed paper over it. Place the stack of phyllo on this and then cover it with another sheet of waxed paper, followed by another damp towel.

To assemble: brush the bottom and sides of the baking dish with melted butter. Begin by laying a sheet of phyllo in the pan. Turn bottom ends over if it is too long. Brush it with butter and repeat until 25 sheets cover the bottom of the pan. End with a buttered sheet on top. Evenly sprinkle the nut mixture over the bottom and press down with the back of a spoon or your hand. Continue layering the remaining phyllo sheets with butter between each sheet. End with buttered sheet on top. Cut, unbaked, pastry into 1 inch diamond shapes by cutting on the diagonal. This will result in triangular shaped pieces around the edges of the pan.

Bake in a preheated oven at 325 degrees for 1 hour or until it is golden brown. After cooling slightly, pour about 2/3 of syrup over the entire pan's contents. Cover loosely with waxed paper. Pour the remaining syrup over the top the next day. Serve individual pieces of baklava in it's own paper cup (muffin pan liners). Store leftovers at room temperature with a loosely fitted cover. Do not refrigerate or freeze. ALTERNATE LAYERING METHOD: After layering 12 sheets with butter brushed between each, sprinkle about 1/3 of the nut ;mixture. Continue layering until all of the nuts are used. Layer remaining sheets of phyllo (about 25) on top and end with a buttered surface.

"This authentic Greek recipe was demonstrated to me by my friend, Marian Siersbeck, a retired Home Economics teacher, whose mother brought it with her from Greece. My students and family have enjoyed it for many years."

Mary Ellen Kile   **Edison High School, Huntington Beach, CA**

VIENNESE ALMOND TORTE

Serves 12   EUROPE

Crust:
2 cups Pillsbury BEST All Purpose or
*   Unbleached Flour*
1/2 cup brown sugar, firmly packed

1/2 to 1 teaspoon cardamom
1/2 cup butter or margarine

filling:
2/3 cup sugar
1/2 cup butter or margarine, melted
3 eggs
1/2 teaspoon almond extract

1 cup vanilla milk chips or 6 ounces
*   white baking bar, coarsely chopped*
1 1/2 cups almonds, sliced, divided
powdered sugar, if desired

Heat oven to 400 degrees. Lightly spoon flour into measuring cup; level off. In medium bowl, combine flour, brown sugar and cardamom; mix well. Using pastry blender or fork, cut in ½ cup butter until mixture is crumbly* (Mixture will be dry.) Press 1¾ cups crumbs in bottom and 1" up sides of 9" or 10" ungreased springform pan. Bake for 10 - 12 minutes or until light golden brown. Remove from oven and reduce heat to 350 degrees.

In a large bowl, combine sugar, melted butter, eggs and almond extract; blend well. Stir in vanilla milk chips and 1 cup almonds; mix well. Pour into crust lined pan. Sprinkle with remaining crumbs. Sprinkle 1/2 cup almonds around edge of torte. Bake for 40 to 55 minutes, until golden brown and nuts are lightly toasted. (Place foil or cookie sheet on lowest rack during baking to guard against spillage.) Remove from oven and cool 10 minutes. Run knife around sides of pan to loosen; remove sides of pan. Sprinkle lightly with powdered sugar. Serve warm or cool.

NOTE: To prepare crust in food processor, combine all crust ingredients in food processor bowl with metal blade. Process 10 to 15 seconds or until mixture is crumbly.

The Pillsbury Co. **Minneapolis, MN**

ITALIAN COCONUT CREAM CAKE

Serves 12 - 16 **ITALY**

2 cups sugar
1/2 pound butter, divided
5 egg yolks
1/2 cup shortening
2 cups flour
1 teaspoon baking soda
1 cup buttermilk

1/2 cup pecans, chopped
2 cups shredded coconut
2 teaspoons vanilla, divided
5 egg whites, stiffly beaten
8 ounces cream cheese
1 pound powdered sugar

Cream together sugar, 1/4 pound butter, egg yolks and shortening. Add flour, baking soda, buttermilk, pecans, coconut, and 1 teaspoon vanilla. Stir to blend well. Fold into beaten egg whites. Pour into 3 cake pans that have been coated with shortening and dusted with flour. Bake at 350 degrees for 25 to 35 minutes. For Icing: Cream together 1/4 pound butter, cream cheese, powdered sugar and 1 teaspoon vanilla. Ice only top and center of cakes (leaving sides plain). Sprinkle top with toasted coconut if desired.

"This recipe came to me from my high school Home Economics teacher, Bonnie Rose. It is the best cake I've ever had. My friends beg for this recipe!"

Monica Carlson **La Contenta Junior High School, Yucca Valley, CA**

CARROT CAKE

Serves 20 **GERMANY**

3 cups carrots, grated
1 cup walnuts, chopped
2 cups granulated sugar
1 1/2 cups oil
4 eggs
1 1/2 teaspoons cinnamon
1 teaspoon salt
2 teaspoons baking powder
1 1/2 teaspoons baking soda

1 (7 or 8 ounce) can crushed
pineapple,
    undrained
2 cups flour
1 (8 ounce) package cream cheese,
    softened
1 cube butter, softened
1 (1 pound) box powdered sugar
1/2 cups nuts, chopped (optional)

Mix first 11 ingredients together. Pour into a greased and floured 13" x 19" baking pan. Bake at 350 degrees for 45 minutes. Combine cream cheese, butter, powdered sugar and nuts together and beat until smooth. Spread on top of cooled cake.

"A favorite of students at our Harvest Dinner."

Darlene Lupul **Tokay High School, Lodi, CA**

ITALIAN CASSATA

Serves 6 - 8   **ITALY**

1 (16 ounce) pound cake
16 ounces ricotta cheese
4 ounces semi-sweet chocolate chips,
*   chopped*

3 tablespoons vanilla or orange-
*   flavored liquer*
1/4 cup sugar
12 maraschino cherries, chopped

<u>*Chocolate Frosting:*</u>
2 1/2 cups powdered sugar
1/3 cup margarine, softened
2 ounces unsweetened chocolate,
*   melted*

2 teaspoons instant coffee
3 tablespoons hot water

Cut pound cake horizontally into 4 equal slices. Combine remaining ingredients in a bowl. Evenly spread ricotta mixture over layers, topping each with another layer of cake. Reassemble cake; cover with plastic wrap and refrigerate while preparing frosting. To prepare frosting: beat powdered sugar, margarine and chocolate in a small mixer bowl on low speed. Dissolve instant coffee in hot water. Add coffee gradually to chocolate mixture, beating until smooth and creamy. If necessary, stir in additional water, a few drops at a time. Frost top and sides of cake. Chill.

"This was a big hit in our Italian Foods unit, and it's very easy."
Penny Niadna   **Golden West High School, Visalia, CA**

ITALIAN PIZZELLE

Makes 2 dozen   **ITALY**

3 eggs
3/4 cup sugar
3/4 cup margarine

3/4 to 1 cup flour
1 teaspoon anise extract
1 teaspoon vanilla

Add and beat together ingredients in order listed (use a smaller amount of flour for thinner pizzelle). Batter should be thick when flowing from a spoon. Place about 1 tablespoon of batter in center of both sections of preheated grid. Close lid. Allow to cook until steaming stops, about 45 to 60 seconds. Remove with fork. Allow to cool on a wire rack or towels.

NOTE: While hot, they may be rolled into cylinder or shaped into a cone. Dust with powdered sugar.

"To make this cookie you need a waffle iron with special Pizzelle grid or special grid that may be used on top of a stove."
Karen McCord   **Lindsay High School, Lindsay, CA**

CORNUCOPIAS

Makes 24   **ENGLAND**

2 eggs, slightly beaten
1/2 cup sugar
2/3 cups flour, sifted

1/4 teaspoon vanilla
1 tablespoon water

Armenian Turkey Dumplings, Page 130

Russian Chicken with Gooseberry Sauce, Page 54

Taquitos al Pastor, Page 123

Blend all ingredients together using a mixer. Drop by tablespoonfuls onto greased cookie sheet. Bake. Immediately after removing from oven, lift with turner and roll one side to form a funnel shape (cone). Let cool. Fill with your choice of: vanilla pudding with chopped bananas, chocolate pudding, whipped cream mixed with drained fruit cocktail, or ice cream.

"A delightful cookie to be served with tea."

Sonja Tyree   **Ayala High School, Chino Hills, CA**

ITALIAN ALMOND NUT BISCOTTI

Makes 4 -5 dozen   **ITALY**

1 cup flour
1 cup sugar
1 teaspoon baking powder
1 teaspoon cinnamon
1/2 teaspoon nutmeg
1 cup walnuts, chopped

1 cup almonds, chopped
1 teaspoon vanilla
2 eggs, well beaten
1/2 cup vegetable oil
6 ounces semi-sweet chocolate
*   (for dipping), optional*

Mix all dry ingredients and nuts together. Beat vanilla, eggs and vegetable oil together and add to dry ingredients. Mix together. Knead until dough is smooth and manageable. Roll dough into oblong cookie loaves 5 inches broad and about 3/4 inches thick. Make sure you have plenty of flour on kneading board when forming cookie loaves. Place loaves on, greased, cookie sheets. Bake at 350 degrees for 12 minutes. Remove from oven. Slice cookie loaves at an angle about one inch thick. Return cookie slices side up to the oven and bake for 5 minutes. Turn cookie slices over and bake for 5 minutes more. Place on cookie racks to cool. Store in an airtight tin. Option: Melt chocolate pieces in a double boiler set over simmering water. Dip the long bottom edge of each cookie into melted chocolate. Place cookie on a baking sheet lined with wax paper. Refrigerate until chocolate is set, about 15 minutes.

Angela Croce   **Mira Mesa High School, San Diego, CA**

ANISE BISCUITS

Makes 36   **ITALY**

1 cup sugar
1/2 cup butter
3 eggs (reserve 1 yolk)
1 teaspoon anise extract
1 teaspoon anise seed

3 cups all-purpose flour
1/2 teaspoon salt
2 teaspoons baking powder
1 tablespoon milk
multi-colored sprinkles (optional)

Cream sugar and butter. Add eggs (reserving 1 yolk) and beat well. Stir in anise extract and anise seeds. Combine flour, salt and baking powder. Thoroughly blend into sugar and egg mixture. On greased baking sheets, form dough into two long flat loaves 1/2" thick by 2" wide. Combine reserved yolk and 1 tablespoon milk, brush over top of loaves. Sprinkle with multi-colored sprinkles, if desired. Bake at 375 degrees for 20 minutes. Remove from oven and cool slightly. Cut into 1" diagonal slices. Replace on baking sheets, cut side down, and return to oven. Bake for 5 minutes on each side or until golden. After cooling on wire racks, store in airtight containers.

"A favorite for dunking into wine or coffee; can be saved a while if stored in airtight containers. This is actually a favorite recipe from Mark Aiassa, our Art teacher, who is also an excellent cook!"

Gaylen Roe   **Magnolia Junior High School, Chino, CA**

QUICK TORTONI

Serves 6   **ITALY**

1 1/2 cups vanilla ice cream
3 tablespoons macaroon cookie
* crumbs*
1 teaspoon rum extract

1 tablespoon diced maraschino
* cherries*
1 tablespoon blanched almonds,
* chopped*

Soften ice cream in a bowl with a wooden spoon. Add remaining ingredients. Mix. Place in individual fluted paper cups. Top with piece of cherry. Freeze.

Note: You may take out of paper cup and serve in a dish or eat from the paper cup - like an ice cream bar.

"Our favorite choice to follow pizza - one of the student's favorite meals!"

Susie Pendleton   **Cerritos High School, Cerritos, CA**

ENGLISH SHORTBREAD

Serves 15   **ENGLAND**

4 cups all purpose flour
1 1/4 cups confectioners sugar

1 teaspoon baking powder
2 cups butter, softened

Preheat oven to 325 degrees. Measure all dry ingredients in large bowl. Work the butter into the dry mixture until well blended. Knead gently until mixture forms a soft dough. Pat evenly into 2 9" round or 30 small tart pans. Bake for 40 minutes or until light golden brown. Store in tightly covered containers.

"Wrapped in cellophane and tied with ribbons, these shortbreads make delicious Christmas presents for friends and neighbors."

Betty Wells   **Oroville High School, Oroville, CA**

NANA'S SCOTTISH SHORTBREAD

Makes 24 - 36   **SCOTLAND**

1/2 cup sugar
1/2 cup butter, softened

1/2 cup rice flour
2 cups all purpose flour

Work sugar into softened butter, then add rice flour and work it in. Last, add all purpose flour. Work with your hands; the heat from your hands helps make it smooth. Pat to 1/2" thick. Cut into any shape or size desired. Bake in a 300 degree oven for 20 to 30 minutes, or until very light brown.

"Brought from Aberdeen, Scotland in 1909 by my great grandmother, Isabella Mackie Porter Knight. These will melt in your mouth. A family favorite."

Laura May   **Hesperia Junior High School, Hesperia, CA**

CHIAMELL (TEA BISCUIT)

Makes 3 dozen   ITALY

Topping:
1/4 cup sugar   *1 tablespoon cinnamon*

Dough:
1 cup oil   *1 egg*
1 cup sugar   *1 tablespoon anise seed*
1 cup white wine   *4 - 5 cups flour, as needed*

Combine topping ingredients together and set aside. Mix oil, sugar, wine, egg and anise seed with mixer in bowl. Add flour, one cup at a time until you can't stir any longer. Turn onto floured surface. Knead dough and add flour, as needed, for about 5 minutes or until not sticky any longer. Slice off 1" at a time and roll in a long rope, the thickness of your thumb. Cut length into 6" rope. Twist rope into desired shape. Still holding onto end, slit 3 places along edge. Dip top into topping mixture. Put on, ungreased, cookie sheet about 1/4" apart. Bake at 325 degrees for 25 to 30 minutes.

"This has been a family favorite. Biscuits are supposed to be a little hard."

Ruth Schletewitz   Rafer Johnson Junior High School, Kingsburg, CA

QUICK PIZZA STICKS

Serves 8   ITALY

1 (11 ounce) can Pillsbury Soft   *24 thin pepperoni slices*
* Bread Sticks*   *1 cup mozzarella cheese, shredded*
1/2 cup pizza sauce   *1/2 cup Parmesan cheese*

Separate and unroll bread sticks. Place 1 tablespoon pizza sauce on half of the breadstick (you may want to flatten this half of the breadstick a little). Place 3 pieces of pepperoni on top of sauce. Sprinkle mozzarella cheese on top of pepperoni. Fold remaining half of breadstick over top, seal ends and twist. Place on ungreased cookie sheet. Sprinkle Parmesan cheese on top and bake at 350 degrees for 15 to 20 minutes.

"This is an easy and quick appetizer. You had better have plenty because they disappear fast. Also, you can serve with hot pizza sauce to dip into if you want."

Karen Tilson   Poly High School, Riverside, CA

GERMAN APPLE CAKE

Serves 12   GERMANY

1 package German chocolate cake mix   *3 eggs*
2 cups prepared apple pie filling   *whipped cream (for topping)*

In a large bowl, combine cake mix, apple pie filling and eggs. Beat with electric mixer for 2 minutes on medium speed, scraping sides of bowl. Pour into a 13" x 9" pan that has been greased (with butter or margarine) and dusted with flour. Bake at 350 degrees for 40 to 50 minutes. Cool cake completely. To serve, top with whipped cream (add a little bit of cinnamon if desired).

"This makes a wonderful dessert during Oktoberfest!!"

Tricia Bergmann-Montelongo   South Junior High School, Anaheim, CA

INDIA

The cuisine of India is as complex as the people. Scores of cooking methods and flavoring ingredients divide it into many important provincial styles. Ancient ways are a part of life in India and this applies also to the cooking.

The most common ingredient associated with Indian food is curry. Contrary to American belief, curry is not a single spice, but a blend of many spices and herbs, usually made fresh every day in individualistic fashion by Indian housewives and cooks. The original word in Hindustani is turcarri, and it could consist of many combinations such as coriander, poppy seeds, ground almonds, cloves, ginger, salt and chili. Foods seasoned in this way may be spicy or hot, but are often mild or even sweet.

India

CALCUTTA CHICKEN SALAD

Serves 10 - 12   INDIA

1 cup coconut, shredded
1 cup raisins, steamed
1 cup unsalted peanuts, chopped
1 cup banana, (barely ripe), diced
1 cup red apple, unpeeled and diced
1 cup pineapple (juice packed, NOT
sugar packed or fresh), diced
1 cup celery, sliced

2 cups cooked chicken, shredded
1 cup chutney
1 cup mayonnaise
2 tablespoons curry powder
lettuce, cantaloupe, grapes
and 5 piece coconut for garnish

Stir together all ingredients, except garnishes, very gently, smoothing out top. Cover with plastic wrap and refrigerate overnight. Serve on lettuce lined plate or on circles of peeled cantaloupe with lettuce leaves. Garnish as desired. Serve as a main dish with bread.

"This wonderful salad is served at the Steinbeck House in Salinas where John Steinbeck was born."

Sheryl Malone   **Mt. Carmel High School, San Diego, CA**

INDIA RELISH

Makes 5 pints   INDIA

<u>*Vegetables - step 1:*</u>
5 1/2 cups cucumbers, peeled &
coarsely chopped (8 medium)
1 2/3 cups sweet green peppers, cored &
seeded, corasely chopped (1 pound)

1 2/3 cups onions, chopped
medium-fine (3 medium)
6 tablespoons coarse Kosher salt

<u>*Vegetables - step 2:*</u>
3 cups cabbage, chopped medium-fine

<u>*Pickling spices:*</u>
1 cup light brown sugar, firmly packed
3 cups cider vinegar
1/2 cup light corn syrup
2 tablespoons mustard seeds
1 teaspoon celery seed

1/2 teaspoon tumeric
1/2 tesapoon ground black pepper
1/2 tesapoon ground ginger
1/4 tesapoon ground mace

<u>*Seasonings:*</u>
1 tablespoon dry mustard
1/2 teaspoon curry powder

1 small clove garlic, minced to a paste
2 tablespoons olive or vegetable oil

Step 1: Combine vegetable ingredients with salt (step 1) in a ceramic glass or stainless steel bowl and let stand from 6 - 12 hours.

Step 2: Drain the salted vegetables and put into a large bowl. Mix in chopped cabbage (step 2).

Step 3: In a stainless steel or enameled kettle, combine the pickling spices and boil for 1 to 2 minutes, then pour over vegetables. Stir and let stand for 3 hours. Strain the pickling liquid back into the kettle, keeping out 1/2 cup. Step 4: Combine the 1/2 cup liquid with remaining ingredients (seasonings), stirring until smooth. Add to the liquid in the preserving pot and bring to a boil. Return the vegetables to the pot; bring just to a full boil, stirring the vegetables from the sides toward the center so they heat uniformly. Ladle the relish into hot, clean pint or 1/2 pint canning jars, leaving 1/2" headspace. Cover with 2-piece lids or fasten screw bands. Put jars on rack in deep kettle half full of water to cover lids by 2 inches. Bring to a hard boil; cover, boil 5 minutes. Cool. Mellow for 1 month.

"This is an involved recipe and takes time, but the results are WONDERFUL! It was given to me by my friend, Ruth. A great gift to make ahead."

Charla Rayl   **Fallbrook High School, Fallbrook, CA**

INDIAN PILAF

Serves 6 - 8   **INDIA**

1 tablespoons margarine	*1/2 teaspoon turmeric*
1/2 cup onion, chopped	*1/4 teaspoon curry powder*
1 1/2 cup rice, uncooked	*1/8 teaspoon pepper*
1/2 teaspoon salt	*3 1/2 cups chicken broth*
1/2 teaspoon allspice	*1/4 cup blanched almonds, slivered*

Melt margarine in large skillet. Add onion and rice. Stir to cook evenly until onion is transparent and rice is yellow. Stir in the salt, allspice, turmeric, curry powder and pepper. Pour into a 2 quart casserole with a tight-fitting lid and set aside. Heat chicken broth to boiling. Add broth to rice in casserole. Cover and bake at 350 degrees for 40 minutes or until liquid is absorbed and rice is tender. Sprinkle with almonds.

"I serve this with all types of baked chicken recipes."

Alice Demele   **Colton High School, Colton, CA**

CURRY RICE

Serves 6 -8   **INDIA**

3 cups chicken, cooked and diced	*1/2 teaspoon mace*
1 1/2 cups rice	*1/2 teaspoon ginger*
1/4 cup margarine	*1 cup light cream*
3/4 cup flour	*1/2 cup applesauce*
1 tablespoon curry	*2 cups chicken broth*
1 teaspoon salt	*1 cup chicken gel*
1/2 teaspoon allspice	*cayenne pepper, to taste*

<u>*Toppings:*</u>

3/4 cup chutney
3/4 cup raisins
2 bananas, chopped
peanuts, chopped
coconut

celery
1/2 pound bacon, crumbled
6 hard cooked eggs, chopped
2 apples, chopped
2 onions, chopped

2 tomatoes, chopped
1 small jar marmalade

1 large green pepper, chopped
1 can black olives, chopped

Cook chicken and set aside. Cook rice and set aside. Melt margarine and add flour. When mixture is smooth, add spices and liquid ingredients gradually; simmer until thickened. Add chicken and cayenne pepper to taste. Serve over rice and top with any or all of the toppings.

"A great recipe for a dinner party. Have all the guests bring the toppings. This Americanized version is NOT hot and is easily doubled or tripled for a crowd. Credit goes to a teacher-friend, Marcia Taylor."

Joan Goodell   **Eldorado High School, Las Vegas, NV**

CHICKEN CURRY OVER RICE

Serves 6 - 8   **INDIA**

3 large chicken breasts, skinned and
*   boned*
2 1/2 cups plain yogurt
1 (10 ounce) jar PATAKS mild curry
*   paste**
1 (10 ounce) jar PATAKS Madras
*   (medium hot) curry paste**
1 onion, chopped
5 cloves garlic, minced

8 tomatoes, chopped
1/2 teaspoon fresh ginger
dash of fennel seed
2 potatoes, boiled and peeled
16 ounces frozen or canned vegetables
*   of your choice*
1 tablespoon garam masala*
small amount of ghee* or oil or butter
*   (for sauteeing)*

*These items may be found in a Middle Eastern food store.

Precook chicken; shred and marinate in 1 1/2 cups yogurt and 3 tablespoons mild curry paste. Saute onion and garlic in large pot. Add tomatoes, ginger and fennel to sauteed mixture. Add 1/2 of 10 ounce bottle mild curry paste. Simmer until tomatoes are softened. Add potatoes, vegetables, chicken mixture and 1 cup yogurt. Add 3 tablespoons hot curry paste. Simmer 1 hour. Add 1 tablespoon garam masala and simmer 5 minutes. Serve over rice with naan (Indian bread).

"This is my son's recipe! He loves to experiment with and create new dishes."

Carolyn Cummings   **Newhart Middle School, Mission Viejo, CA**

CURRY CHICKEN

Serves 4 - 6

2 pounds chicken, boneless, skinless   1 - 3 tablespoons oil
salt, to taste   3 tablespoons cornstarch
pepper, to taste   1 1/2 cups water
curry powder, to taste   1/4 cup onion, finely chopped
garlic powder or salt, to taste

Wash chicken and remove skin. Season to taste with salt, pepper, curry powder and garlic powder. Cook chicken in skillet in oil, turning 2 to 4 times. (Skinless chicken will stick if you don't turn it.) Combine cornstarch and water; set aside. Pour off fat; add onion and cornstarch mixture. Cover and cook over medium heat until juices from chicken run clear when pierced with fork. Serve with rice seasoned with 1/2 package GOYDA seasoning.

"This dish has a mild spicy flavor and taste better served as leftovers over steamed rice."

Jannie Parks   **Ramona High School, Riverside, CA**

DATE TORTE W/RUM HARD SAUCE

Serves 6   INDIA

2 eggs + 1 egg yolk (from Hard Sauce),   1 teaspoon baking powder
    well beaten   1/2 teaspoon salt
1/2 cup sugar   1' cup dates, chopped
1/3 cup flour   1 cup walnuts, chopped

Rum Hard Sauce:
1/4 cup butter
1 cup powdered sugar
1 egg white, beaten stiff
1 teaspoon rum flavoring

Beat 2 eggs and egg yolk adding sugar slowly. Sift together flour, baking powder and salt and add to eggs and sugar. Add dates and nuts. Pour into a greased and floured 8 inch Pyrex pie pan and bake slowly at 250 degrees for 40 minutes. (If lightly browned, it will be chewy - if it is cooked too fast, it will be brittle and too crisp to eat.) Prepare Hard Sauce: cream butter and powdered sugar. Add to stiffly beaten egg white. Add rum flavoring and beat thoroughly together. While soft, put in serving dish to harden.

"A very rich dessert brought into my mother's family via English army officers stationed in India."

Sue Walters   **Morse High School, San Diego, CA**

THE ISLANDS

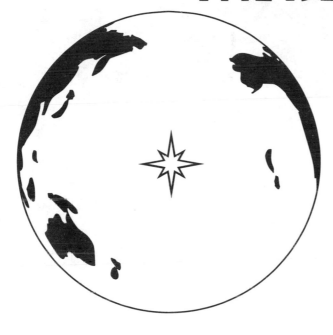

Guam
Hawaii
Jamaica
Philippines
Polynesia

Island people have traditionally formed their diet from fish and native plants. The shallow water fish are crabs, lobsters, shrimp and turtles. The deep sea fish they rely on are tuna and bonito. Breadfruit, coconut palms and pandanus trees characterize many of the islands. Not only is the fruit eaten, but the leaves and fibers of such plants are used to weave baskets and mats.

The distinction of Philippine cooking is the strong Spanish influence stemming from 400 years of Spanish rule. It is not surprising that rice is a part of every meal in the Philippines, since it is one of the world's chief producers. Fish is the second item of importance in the Philippine diet, milkfish being a favorite.

Conjure in your mind the image of a whole pig roasting over a charcoal fire, and you have the popular dish known as lechon. The meal is complimented with an alcoholic beverage derived from the sap of coconut palm blossoms.

THE ISLANDS

HAWAIIAN BREAD

Makes 4 loaves   **HAWAII**

3 cups sugar
4 eggs
1 cup oil
2 cups pumpkin
3 1/2 cups flour
2 teaspoons baking soda
2 teaspoons nutmeg

1 1/2 teaspoons salt
2 teaspoons cinnamon
1/2 teaspoon allspice
1 cup pineapple, crushed
1 cup walnuts, chopped
1 cup coconut, shredded

Mix together sugar, eggs, oil and pumpkin. In a medium bowl, sift together flour baking soda, salt and spices; add to pumpkin mixture. Add pineapple, walnuts and coconut and mix for 2 minutes. Pour batter into 4 - l pound greased and floured loaf pans and bake at 350 degrees for 1 hour, or until toothpick inserted into center comes out clean.

"This is a recipe that was entered in a pumpkin recipe contest that I judged. Yummy!"

Pat Dallas   **Westminster High School, Westminster, CA**

KELEQUIN (SPICY CHICKEN SALAD)

Serves 4 - 6   **GUAM**

4 - 5 pounds chicken pieces (breasts,
*   thighs and drumsticks)*
2 bunches green onion, minced
3 - 4 lemons, squeezed for fresh juice
garlic salt to taste

salt and pepper to taste
1 to 2 jalapeño peppers, roasted and
*   minced*
2 dozen flour tortillas

Broil chicken, debone and mince. Combine all ingredients in a large bowl, adding lemon juice and seasonings slowly to taste as you go. Chill salad and serve in tortillas.

"Recipe is a family favorite. It came from my husband's family, many of which still live in Guam. It's great tasting and low in calories."

Connie Sweet   **Rim of the World High School, Lake Arrowhead, CA**

POLYNESIAN MEATBALLS

Serves many   POLYNESIA

Meatballs:
3 pounds lean ground beef   *1/2 teaspoon salt*
2 cups quick cooking oats   *2 tablespoons soy sauce*
1 medium can water chestnuts, chopped   *2 eggs*
1 teaspoon onion salt   *1 cup milk*
1 teaspoon garlic salt

Sauce:
1 (16 ounce) can pineapple tidbits   *3/4 cup vinegar*
2 cups brown sugar   *4 teaspoons soy sauce*
1/4 cup cornstarch   *1 cup green pepper, chopped*
2 cubes beef bouillon

Meatballs: mix all ingredients together and form into small balls. Place on a cookie sheet and bake at 375 degrees until done about 25 - 25 minutes.Sauce: Save pineapple juice. Mix sugar and cornstarch. Add juice, bouillon, vinegar and soy sauce. Boil until mixture is thickened. Stir in green pepper and pineapple chunks. Pour over meatballs and simmer at least 1/2 hour. Stir to coat meatballs. May be kept in crockpot while serving.

"Great to have cooked meatballs frozen. All you have to do is cook the sauce while thawing meatballs and heat until ready to serve."

Paula Schaefer   **Garside Middle School, Las Vegas, NV**

BAKED SPARERIBS ALOHA

Serves 4   HAWAII

3 pounds country style pork spareribs   *1/2 teaspoon dry mustard*
salt and pepper, to taste   *2 1/2 cups pineapple tidbits, with juice*
1/2 cup onion, chopped   *2 (8 ounce) cans tomato sauce*
1/2 cup green pepper, chopped   *1 tablespoon worcestershire sauce*
1/4 cup brown sugar   *1/2 cup vinegar*

Cut ribs into serving pieces; sprinkle with salt and pepper and place in a shallow baking dish. Bake at 450 degrees for 1/2 hour; pour off excess fat. Reduce oven heat to 350 degrees. Mix remaining ingredients and pour over ribs. Bake for 1 1/2 hours, basting frequently.

"My mother gave me this recipe about 20 years ago and it has been one of my husband's favorites ever since."

Denise Thomas   **Matilija Junior High School, Ojai, CA**

ED´S SPARERIBS

Serves 5 - 6   HAWAII

3 pounds spareribs   *2 tablespoons mirin (sweet rice wine)*
1/2 cup sugar   *1/2 cup soy sauce*
1 cup ketchup   *1/4 cup oyster sauce*
1 teaspoon fresh ginger, grated

Cut spareribs into individual pieces. Boil ribs in a large pot with enough water to cover, for about 45 minutes. Drain water. Place ribs in a baking pan in a single layer. Combine other ingredients and mix well. Pour over ribs; marinate for 1 hour. Bake in 300 degrees for 1 hour, until browned.

"A family favorite!"

Reiko Ikkanda   **South Pasadena Middle School, South Pasadena, CA**

HAWAIIAN PORK

Serves 6   **HAWAII**

3 - 4 cups roasted pork, cubed
2 cans pineapple chunks, reserve juice
2 tablespoons soy sauce
1/4 cup brown sugar
1/3 cup white vinegar
3 tablespoons corn starch

2 green peppers, cut into bite-size
   pieces
1 medium mild onion, thin sliced
   into rings
2 cups long grain rice, cooked
   according to package directions

Cut roasted pork into cubes about 3/4" to 1" square. Combine juice from pineapple, soy sauce, brown sugar, vinegar and cornstarch; simmer over low heat, stirring constantly until sweet and sour sauce is thick and shiny. Pour over meat; let stand 10 to 30 minutes. Add onion rings, pineapple chunks and bell pepper; cook until onion and pepper are tender but not overcooked. Serve over rice.

"This is my mother-in-law's choice for birthdays, Mother's Day, etc."

Deanne Moody   **Monte Vista High School, Spring Valley, CA**

CHICKEN ADOBO

Serves 6   **PHILLIPINES**

1 large chicken, cut up
1/4 cup vinegar
1/4 cup soy sauce
3 cloves garlic, crushed

2 bay leaves, broken in half
2 tablespoons oil
water
salt and pepper

Cut roasted pork into cubes about 3/4" to 1" square. Combine juice from pineapple, soy sauce, brown sugar, vinegar and cornstarch; simmer over low heat, stirring constantly until sweet and sour sauce is thick and shiny. Pour over meat; let stand 10 to 30 minutes. Add onion rings, pineapple chunks and bell pepper; cook until onion and pepper are tender but not overcooked. Serve over rice.

Chicken Adobo: Combine vinegar, soy sauce, garlic and bay leaves in a large bowl. Marinate chicken in mixture for at least 1 hour. Drain; reserving marinade. In a Dutch oven, heat oil. Brown chicken in oil; drain. Remove oil; add reserved marinade and enough water to cover chicken . Season to taste with salt and pepper. Bring to a boil, then simmer on low, covered, for 1 hour. Uncover and continue cooking for 15 minutes. Serve with rice.

"Thanks to my dear friend, Susie McLellen, for sharing this recipe. Easy and delicious."

Mary Rector   **Valley High School, Las Vegas, NV**

JAMAICAN CHICKEN

Serves 4   JAMAICA

1 medium onion, chopped
1 clove garlic
2 tablespoons crushed red pepper
1/3 cup soy sauce
1/4 cup vinegar
2 tablespoons dark brown sugar
1/2 teaspoon black pepper

1/4 teaspoon ground ginger
1/4 teaspoon ground cinnamon
1/2 teaspoon thyme leaves
1 pound boneless chicken breast or
     thighs, cut into 1 inch cubes
lime wedges, for garnish

Blend first ten ingredients in food blender until smooth. Place chicken in 1 layer in a 9 inch microwave- safe dish. Pour sauce over chicken, turning pieces to coat. Cover dish and microwave on High (100%) power for 6 to 8 minutes, or until juices run clear, turning pieces half way through cooking time. To serve, spoon chicken with sauce over "Spiced Rice" and garnish with lime wedges.

Jeanette Woll   Antelope Valley High School, Antelope Valley, CA

ORANGE ALMOND CHICKEN

Serves 4 - 6   POLYNESIA

8 half chicken breasts, deboned
     & skinned
1 teaspoon salt
1/2 teaspoon pepper
1 teaspoon ginger
1/2 cup flour (approx.)
1/4 cup butter or margarine

6 tablespoons almonds, sliced
1 (11 ounce) can mandarin oranges
1 - 2 tablespoons sugar
dash of ground cloves
juice of 1 lemon
1 cup beef stock
1 teaspoon cornstarch

Sprinkle chicken with mixture of salt, pepper, ginger and flour. Slowly fry chicken in butter until both sides are brown; remove from frypan and set aside. Add almonds to frypan and saute until golden brown. Drain mandarin oranges, reserving juice. Add oranges, sugar, ground cloves, lemon juice and beef stock to almonds. Simmer until liquid is reduced by one half. Blend cornstarch with mandarin orange juice and stir into almond sauce. Continue to cook until thickened. Add chicken to sauce. Cover and simmer 15-20 minutes or until done. Serve over a bed of steamed white or brown rice.

"A personal favorite I got when working at Southern California Edison Company."
Patty Dyle   John F. Kennedy High School, La Palma, CA

HAWAIIAN BAKED ALASKA

Serves 2   HAWAII

1 pineapple, fresh
ice cream (vanilla, chocolate,
     strawberry or an assortment)
3 egg whites

1/4 teaspoon cream of tartar
1/2 teaspoon vanilla
6 tablespoons sugar
2 tablespoons powdered sugar

Cut pineapple in half lengthwise, scoop out fruit at the center, leaving the sidewalls about 1/2 inch thick; place on platter and set aside. Cut pineapple fruit into bite-sized pieces. Fill pineapple cavity with ice cream and place in freezer until ice cream is solid. In a clean bowl, beat egg whites with cream of tartar and vanilla until soft peaks form. Gradually add sugar, beating until stiff peaks for, about 3 minutes. Remove pineapple from freezer and place desired amount of fruit on top of ice cream. Cover ice cream entirely with meringue, creating a decorative design (you may use a star tube tip to create design). Dust with powdered sugar and brown quickly in a 450 degree oven. Serve immediately.

Karen Tilson   **Poly High School, Riverside, CA**

MACADAMIA NUT CREAM PIE

Serves 6 - 8   **HAWAII**

1 9 inch pastry shell, baked	*2 tablespoons butter*
1 cup sugar	*1/2 teaspoon vanilla*
4 tablespoons cornstarch	*1 teaspoon kahlua*
1/4 teaspoon salt	*1 cup macadamia nuts, chopped*
3 cups milk	*whipped cream + dash of kahlua*
4 egg yolks, lightly beaten	*for topping*

Combine sugar, cornstarch, salt in a sauce pan. Stir in milk. Stir over medium heat to boil. Cook 2 minutes longer. Remove from heat. Stir a few spoons of hot mixture into egg yolks; return to pan and mix into hot mixture. Cook and stir 2 minutes. Remove from heat and add butter, vanilla and kahlua. Stir in well. Cool to room temperature. Cover bottom of pre-baked pie shell with chopped macadamia nuts. fill shell with cream filling; sprinkle with additional chopped nuts. Top with whipped cream flavored with a dash of kahlua.

NOTE: Use unsalted macadamia nuts or rinse off salt and dry nuts in a warm oven before chopping.

"Many thanks to friends, Bob and Mary Hansen, for sharing this pie during a briefing on my family's first visit to Hawaii."

Gerry Henderson   **Temple City High School, Temple City, CA**

MIDGETS

Serves 15 - 20   **PHILLIPINES**

1 pound ground beef	*pepper to taste*
1 pound ground pork	*1 package won ton wrappers*
1 bunch green onions, chopped	*oil for frying*
garlic salt to taste	

Mix ground beef, ground pork, onions and seasonings together using your hands to mix well. Place a small amount of mixture in won ton wrappers and roll up. Moisten and seal edges of won tons. Heat about 2 inches of oil in a deep skillet and fry each midget until browned, turning occasionally to brown on all sides.

"This recipe was a hit with my 6th period class. One student prepared it as part of a multi-cultural foods unit. It comes from his family."

Cindy Peters   **Park Junior High School, Antioch, CA**

ADOBO

Serves 6

2 pounds 8 ounces chicken drumsticks
3 medium cloves garlic, minced
4 tablespoons soy sauce
3 tablespoon vinegar
1 1/2 cups water

salt and pepper to taste
2 large bay leaves
2 potatoes, cubed
1 tablespoon cornstarch, dissolved in
    1/4 cup water

Place chicken in a large cooking pot. Add all the ingredients except potatoes and cornstarch mixture. After 1/2 hour, when chicken is half done, add the potatoes. Continue cooking for another 1/2 hour. During last 5 minutes, add cornstarch dissolved in water as a thickener.

"A stew with the base of chicken, pork, or beef. This recipe was contributed by Janice Jill Salazar."

Carrie Drewisch   **Vandenberg Middle School, Lompoc, CA**

SPICED RICE

Serves 4   JAMAICA

1 3/4 cup water
1 cup long grain or brown rice
1/2 teaspoon thyme leaves
1/2 teaspoon allspice

1/2 teaspoon cumin
1/2 teaspoon black pepper
1/2 teaspoon Mrs. Dash

Place all ingredients in a microwave-safe 3 quart casserole dish and stir together. Cover tightly and microwave on High (100%) power for 4 to 7 minutes bringing liquid to a boil. Continue to microwave on Medium (50%) power until most of the liquid has been absorbed and the rice is tender, about 10 minutes. Let stand, covered, for 5 minutes more.

Jeanette Woll   **Antelope Valley High School, Antelope Valley, CA**

MEXICO

Mexico derives her culinary origins from a combination of Spanish and Indian cooking. The degrees in which the Spanish influence and the Indian influence are shown in the cooking depends somewhat on how well the available foods adapted to Spanish cooking and how readily the Indians gave in to the Spanish invaders. Ancient Indian cultures, such as the Aztecs and the Mayas, continue to influence Mexican cooking.

Mexico

FRESH MEXICAN SALSA

Serves 4   **MEXICO**

6 green onions, chopped   *1 ripe avocado, cubed*
2 medium tomatoes, chopped   *1 tablespoon fresh lemon juice*
1 small can green chiles   *1 teaspoon garlic salt*
1 tablespoon fresh cilantro, chopped

Combine all ingredients; let sit at least 1 hour for juices to combine. Serve as a sauce for tacos, tostadas, steak or use as a dip with corn chips.

Jane Souza   **North Monterey County High School, Castroville, CA**

LOWFAT BEAN DIP

Makes 5 cups   **MEXICO**

1 (15 ounce) can pinto beans   *1/4 cup green onions, thinly sliced*
1 tablespoon prepared hot sauce   *1 (16 ounce) carton fat-free sour cream*
2 teaspoons lime juice   *1 1/2 cups chunky salsa, drained*
1 tablespoon sugar   *fresh cilantro (optional)*
3 tablespoons chili sauce

Drain liquid from beans and discard. Place the beans in a food processor and process until almost smooth. Add the hot sauce, lime juice, sugar and chili sauce. Mix well. Spread the bean mixture over the bottom of of large platter. Sprinkle the onions evenly over the top. Cover beans and onions with sour cream. Top with salsa. Garnish with cilantro. Serve with tortilla chips.

"This makes a great appetizer. To keep it truly lowfat - bake your own tortilla chips. Cut up corn tortillas into triangles and bake on a baking sheet in a 350 degree oven for 15 minutes, turning once."

Linda Falkenstien   **Morro Bay High School, Morro Bay, CA**

TORTILLA ROLL-UP

Serves 24 MEXICO

24 large flour tortillas (10 inch)
2 pounds Wisconsin Jalapeño Cold
   Pack Cheese
3 pounds chicken pieces, cooked
   and shredded
3 cups mild salsa
1 1/4 pounds red bell pepper,
   seeded and diced

1 1/2 cups scallions or green
   onions, sliced
guacamole, for garnish
sour cream, for garnish
pickled jalapeño peppers, for garnish

Spread each tortilla with 2 to 3 tablespoons Wisconsin Jalapeño Cold Pack Cheese. In bowl, toss chicken with salsa, red pepper and scallions. Spoon approximately 1/2 cup mixture into each tortilla. Roll up tightly. Serve each with black bean salad, salsa and jalapeños. Garnish with guacamole and sour cream, if desired.

Wisconsin Milk Marketing Board   **Madison, WI**

JALAPEÑO ROLL-UPS

Makes 8 - 10 dozen   **MEXICO**

3 (8 ounce) packages cream cheese,
   softened
1 (8 ounce) carton sour cream
2 tablespoons hot picante sauce
1/2 cup onion, finely chopped
2 teaspoons horseradish

1 - 2 tablespoons jalapeños, sliced
juice of one lime
1/2 teaspoon garlic salt
2 - 3 dozen flour tortillas
salsa or picante sauce, for serving

Mix all of the above ingredients (except flour tortillas) together in a bowl until smooth. Spread mixture onto flour tortillas and roll up. Chill at least one hour. Slice and place on serving dish with salsa or picante sauce.

"This recipe came from a colleague at my school. Every time I serve them, they're a hit."

Vicki Pearl   **Giano Intermediate School, La Puente, CA**

MEXICAN PIZZA

Serves 10 - 12   **MEXICO**

1 (1 lb. 14 oz.) can refried beans
1 pound ground beef, cooked
1 pound Jack cheese, grated
2 to 3 green onions, chopped
2 bell pepper, chopped
1/2 (small) can jalapeño peppers,
   chopped

1 (small) can olives, chopped
1 avocado, chopped
2 small tomatoes, chopped
tortilla chips, to serve

On a large pizza pan, layer ingredients in order listed, except avocado and tomatoes. Bake at 350 degrees for 15 to 20 minutes. Remove from oven. Sprinkle with avocado and tomatoes. Serve with tortilla chips.

"To the greatest sister in the world - thank you Margie for everything, including this great recipe! My sister and her husband, Michael Del Puppo, live in Sanger, love Mexican food and this is a favorite family recipe!"

Cheryl McDaniels   **Green Valley High School, Henderson, NV**

POSOLE

Serves 8 - 10   **MEXICO**

3 - 5 pounds pork roast, fat trimmed
1 (29 ounce) can whole tomatoes,
* including juice*
1 large onion, chopped
3 - 4 cloves garlic, chopped
1 tablespoon salt
2 (29 ounce) cans white hominy,
* drained*

Garnishes:
red cabbage, chopped
red onion chopped
cheddar cheese grated
lemon wedges
corn tortillas, fried
salsa

In a large pot, place meat, tomatoes (break tomatoes into small pieces), onion, garlic and salt. Add water to cover about 1 inch above meat. Bring to a boil, then turn down heat and simmer, covered, for 2 - 3 hours or until tender. Remove meat from pan and cut into small pieces. Add back to soup. Add hominy and cook for 1 hour more. Skim fat before serving, or refrigerate overnight to easily remove all fat! (Fat will rise to the top and harden if rcfrigcratcd.)

Serve in bowls with cabbage, onions and cheese on top. Squeeze a lemon wedge into bowl, top with salsa. Use fried tortillas as a scooper or crumble into soup like crackers.

"This is very easy to make and a real crowd pleaser. We often, serve it at football parties. Add a simple dessert and your meal is complete!"

Gail Lambert   **El Rancho Middle School, Anaheim Hills, CA**

SOPA SECA DE FIDEO (DRY SOUP OF VERMICELLI)

Serves 4 - 6   **MEXICO**

1 (8 ounce) package coiled vermicelli,
* broken*
3 tablespoons oil
1/2 small onion, finely chopped
1 clove garlic, minced
1 tablespoon bell pepper, chopped

1 tomato, peeled and chopped
* (or 3 ounces tomato sauce)*
2 cups beef or chicken stock
salt & pepper to taste
Parmesan cheese, for garnish
sour cream, for garnish

Break the vermicelli in short lengths, then brown in hot oil. It is more delicate than rice; do not burn. Drain excess oil. Push the vermicelli to one side, add onion, garlic, bell pepper and cook until onion is soft. Add tomato and mix all together with the vermicelli. Bring the stock to a boil and add to vermicelli mixture. Season to taste. Cover and cook over a very low flame until the liquid is almost completely absorbed. Sprinkle with grated Parmesan cheese and/or a dab of sour cream.

Liz Williams   **Ontario High School, Ontario, CA**

SOUTH OF THE BORDER SOUP

Serves 6 - 8   **MEXICO**

1 pound hamburger
1 (12 ounce) package hot sausage
*   (optional)*
2 cloves garlic, minced
1 small onion, chopped
4 - 5 carrots, sliced
2 cans beef broth + 2 cans water

1 (16 ounce) can tomatoes, undrained,
*   coarsely chopped*
2 cans corn, drained
1/3 cup cilantro, chopped
1/2 teaspoon salt
1/2 teaspoon cumin
serrano chiles, optional

Fry hamburger, sausage, garlic and onion together. When thoroughly cooked, drain all grease off mixture. Combine all ingredients together in a large soup pan and simmer at least an hour. If you like this really spicy, add a couple of chopped serrano chiles. Do NOT eliminate cilantro or cumin. Serve with cornbread or garlic bread.

"I always have a great response to this dish. A keeper!"

Carol Steele   **La Paz Intermediate School, Mission Viejo, CA**

TORTILLA SOUP

Serves 6   **MEXICO**

1/2 pound pinto beans
4 dried chili pods
1 large onion, chopped
1 cup cabbage, chopped
1 cup carrots, sliced
1/2 cup celery, chopped
2 cups tomato sauce
7 corn tortillas
2 cups chicken broth
2 tablespoons chili powder

4 tesapoons cumin
2 tesapoons garlic powder
1 teaspoon onion powder
2 teaspoons salt
1 tablespoon lemon juice
1/2 cup cilantro, chopped
1 cup green onions, chopped
1 pint sour cream
olives, sliced, for garnish

Soak beans overnight. Drain and place in large saucepan; cover with fresh water and simmer until tender (about 45 minutes). Drain. Combine chili pods with 2 cups water and simmer until soft (about 20 minutes). Combine 5 cups water with onion, cabbage, carrots and celery in a large pot and bring to a boil. Reduce heat and simmer 30 minutes. Add beans and tomato sauce. Place cooked chilies with liquid, 4 corn tortillas and chicken broth in blender and blend until smooth. Add to soup. Add chili powder, cumin, garlic powder, onion powder, salt, lemon juice, cilantro and green onions; heat through. Top each serving with dollop of sour cream and garnish with corn tortillas cut into bite-sized triangles and olives.

NOTE: Soup can be pureed in the blender for a really thick and hearty soup.

"This is my daughter's recipe and is a great way to start a meal or for the meal itself!"

Marianne Estes   **La Mirada High School, La Mirada, CA**

FLOUR TORTILLAS

Serves 12   **MEXICO**

2 cups flour
1 1/2 teaspoons baking powder
1/2 teaspoon salt

1/4 cup shortening
1/2 cup + 1 tablespoon warm water

Combine flour, baking powder and salt; cut in shortening. Gradually stir in enough water to form a soft dough. Knead the dough on a lightly floured breadboard until soft and pliable. Divide the dough into 8 equal pieces and shape each into a ball. Roll out into circles about 10" in diameter. Place on preheated griddle or frying pan heated to medium-high heat. Flip to second side when tiny blisters form and tortilla is very lightly browned. Tortilla is done when both sides are lightly browned.

Mary Carr   **Enterprise High School, Redding, CA**

SOPAIPILLAS (PUFFY FRIED BREAD)

Makes 4 dozen   **MEXICO**

4 cups flour, sifted
1 1/2 teaspoons salt
1 teaspoon baking powder
1 tablespoon granulated sugar

1 tablespoon shortening
1 cake compressed yeast
1/4 cup warm water
1/4 cup scalded milk

Combine dry ingredients and cut in shortening. Dissolve yeast in lukewarm water. Add to scalded milk, cooled to room temperature. Make a well in center of dry ingredients. Add liquid to dry ingredients and work into a dough. Knead dough 15 to 20 times and set aside for approximately 10 minutes. Roll dough to 1/4 inch thickness, then cut into triangles and fry in melted shortening that has been heated to 420 degrees. They will puff up and become hollow. Drain on paper towels. Serve as a bread - good with honey.

"This recipe was passed down to me from my Aunt Sophia who was the head of the Foods Dept. for the school district in Santa Fe, New Mexico. We love it!"

Elizabeth Ward   **Norte Vista High School, Riverside, CA**

CRANBERRY SAUCE ALA GUADALAJARA

Serves 6 - 8   **MEXICO**

1 pound fresh cranberries, finely
*   chopped*
2 tart pippin apples, finely chopped
1 cup sugar

1/2 cup orange marmalade
1 (10 ounce) bag frozen raspberries,
*   thawed and drained*
1 teaspoon lemon juice

Combine all ingredients in a bowl and chill at least 1 hour before serving. Fantastic with turkey, over ice cream or just by itself.

"This is the absolute best cranberry sauce. I got it from a little old lady in Guadalajara."

Brenda Burke   **Mt. Whitney High School, Visalia, CA**

CAESAR SALAD

Serves 4   **MEXICO**

Dressing:

1 level teaspoon kosher salt
3/4 teaspoons freshly cracked black &
    white pepper, combined
1/4 teaspoon dry mustard
1 level teaspoon Dijon mustard
1/4 teaspoon granulated sugar

1 teaspoon fresh lemon juice
2 tablespoons tarragon vinegar
2 tablespoons olive oil
6 tablespoons vegetable oil
1 small raw egg, unbeaten
1/2 teaspoons garlic, finely chopped

2 heads romain lettuce, wash and drained
1/2 pound bacon, cut into thin strips, crosswise
3/4 cup croutons
2 tablespoons Parmesan cheese, freshly grated

Combine dressing ingredients in a large wooden bowl in the order given. Stir well with a wooden spoon. (If you are making this in advance, cover bowl with foil.) Set aside. Wash and drain romaine thoroughly, shaking leaves thoroughly in a salad basket to get rid of excess moisture. Separate the leaves, drying each leaf carefully in a towel. Tear the leaves into bite-sized pieces. Put the romaine pieces on top of the dressing .

In a large skillet, fry bacon until crisp; drain. Sprinkle on top of romaine. Sprinkle croutons and Parmesan cheese on top.

When ready to serve: Bring the bowl to the table. Mix the salad thoroughly so the dressing on the bottom coats all of the other ingredients. If you mix it too early, the croutons and bacon will lose their crunchiness, and that is one of the distinctive features of the Caesar Salad.

Note: When this salad is served in restaurants, the headwaiter makes a bit-to-do about adding each ingredient and tossing the final conglomeration. If anyone at your house wants to make a production of it, the bacon, croutons and cheese can be added at the table and the salad tossed with real Hollywood histrionics. It tastes good either way.

"Caesar Salad was created in Tijuana when a popular restaurant ran out of food one Sunday afternoon. Fresh eggs and romaine lettuce were left so a new salad known around the world was created."

Ramona Anderson   **Mira Mesa High School, San Diego, CA**

TACO SALAD

Serves 4 - 6   **MEXICO**

1 head iceberg lettuce
1/2 pound ground beef
1/4 teaspoon garlic powder
1/4 teaspoon salt
1/8 teaspoon pepper
1/2 package corn tortilla chips
1/2 pound cheddar cheese, shredded
1/2 red onion, sliced finely

1/2 basket cherry tomatoes,
  cut in halves
1 (15 ounce) can kidney beans,
  drained and chilled
avocado, peeled and cubed
  (optional)
Ranch dressing or salsa mixed with
  sour cream

Wash and core lettuce; chill. Brown ground beef with seasonings and drain fat. Crush tortilla chips. Reserving several large leaves for garnish, tear remaining lettuce into bite-sized pieces. Toss all ingredients with dressing. Garnish with lettuce leaves.

"This is a favorite of my students when we prepare it in class. We like low-fat sour cream and salsa for dressing. Chicken can also be substituted for beef."

Susan Brown   Sowers Middle School, Huntington Beach, CA

EL GALLO'S MEXICAN RICE

Serves 6   **MEXICO**

3 tablespoons oil
1 clove garlic, chopped
1 cup onion, chopped
1 cup rice
2 cups hot water
2 chicken bouillon cubes

1/4 to 1/2 cup tomato sauce
1 cup chicken, cooked
1 cup corn, canned
salt, to taste
1 tomato, chopped

Heat oil with garlic and onion. Add rice, cook in oil until it turns white, stirring constantly. Add water, bouillon cubes and tomato sauce. Bring to boil. Reduce heat to simmer, add chicken and corn. Season to taste with salt. Cook until most liquid is absorbed. Add tomato and heat through.

"A very good friend gave me his family's recipe for homemade rice."

Laurie Owen   Challenger Junior High School, San Diego, CA

CHICKEN MOLE

Serves 4   **MEXICO**

1/4 cup margarine
6 - 8 chicken drumettes
1/4 cup onion, minced
1 small clove garlic, minced
1 cup tomatoes, cut into small pieces
1 teaspoon beef bouillon dissolved
  in 1/2 cup water
2 teaspoons sugar

1/2 teaspoon chili powder
1/8 teaspoon cinnamon
pinch cloves
pinch nutmeg
dash tabasco sauce
1/4 ounce unsweetened chocolate
1 tablespoon cornstarch dissolved in
  2 tablespoons cold water

Melt margarine in large skillet. Add chicken, onion and garlic. Stir until chicken is browned on all sides, add tomatoes, broth, sugar, chili powder, cinnamon, cloves, nutmeg, tabasco and chocolate. Stir, cover and simmer 15 to 20 minutes. Remove chicken from pan. Stir in cornstarch and water mixture. Simmer 'til thick and bubbly, pour over chicken to serve.

"A great combination of flavors."

Julie Shelburne   **Tulare Union High School, Tulare, CA**

MEXICAN EGGS

Serves 12 - 15   **MEXICO**

1 pound cheddar cheese
1 pound jack cheese
1 (16 ounce) carton sour cream

1 (7 ounce) can Ortega chilies, diced
12 eggs

Preheat oven to 325 degrees. Grate cheese in a bowl. Add sour cream and chilies. Beat eggs and add to cheese mixture. Put mixture in a greased 9" x 13" baking dish. Bake for about 1 hour.

"Although this may not be an authentic Mexican dish, it definitely has a Southwestern flavor. I like to serve it for brunch with salsa, thin sliced ham and rolls or crescents."

Beth Swift   **Buena Park High School, Buena Park, CA**

CHILE RELLENO CASSEROLE

Serves 8   **MEXICO**

1 tablespoon cornmeal
1/2 pound medium-sharp cheddar
*   cheese, grated*
1/2 pound Monterey jack cheese, grated
1 (4 ounce) can green chilies, diced

5 eggs
3/4 cup milk
dash pepper
1/2 teaspoon nutmeg
1 tablespoon wheat germ

Sprinkle cornmeal over bottom of a quiche dish. Cover with one half of the cheese. Sprinkle chilies evenly over cheese and cover with remaining cheeses. Beat eggs, milk and seasonings together. Pour over cheese mixture. Sprinkle with wheat germ. Bake at 350 degrees for 25 to 35 minutes. Allow to set 10 to 15 minutes before serving.

"The cornmeal is a great substitute for a pie crust. Wonderful and easy brunch dish."

Janet Tingley   **Atascadero High School, Atascadero, CA**

CHICKEN TORTILLA CASSEROLE

Serves 6 - 8   **MEXICO**

1 can cream of mushroom soup
1 can cream of chicken soup
1 cup milk
1 small can Ortega salsa sauce

1 teaspoon cumin
1 dozen corn tortillas, cut in 1" strips
6 chicken breasts, cooked and cubed
1 pound sharp cheddar cheese, grated

Combine first 5 ingredients. Dip tortilla strips, a few at a time, in the soup mixture. Layer ingredients in a 9" x 13" casserole dish, beginning with tortilla strips, then chicken, then sauce. Add a layer of cheese. Repeat, ending with grated cheese. Bake at 325 degrees for 1 hour, 35 minutes.

NOTE: May be refrigerated up to 24 hours before baking.

"This has been a family favorite for over 20 years."

Charlotte Runyan   **Saddleback High School, Santa Ana, CA**

CINCO DE MAYO CHICKEN & TORTILLA CASSEROLE

Serves 8   **MEXICO**

3 cups cooked chicken, cut into bite-sized
    pieces OR 6 skinless, boneless
    chicken breasts
1 (16 ounce) jar salsa verde
1 cup light sour cream

1/2 cup half & half
12 corn tortillas
4 cups (1 pound) cheddar cheese,
    shredded
1/3 cup Parmesan cheese, grated

Preheat oven to 350 degrees. Place half the chicken in a 9" x 13" baking pan. Spoon 1/2 of the salsa over chicken. Mix together sour cream and half & half. Mix well and pour over salsa. Cut tortillas into 1/4" wide strips. Top sour cream mixture with half of the tortilla strips and half of the cheddar cheese. Repeat layers. Tightly cover baking pan with foil. Bake 40 minutes, remove foil and sprinkle with Parmesan cheese. Bake uncovered 5 minutes more or until cheese is golden. Let stand 10 minutes before serving.

"Chicken was served at Green & Roman feasts nearly 2,000 years ago. Chicken is rich in protein, iron and B vitamins."

Sandra Hayes   **Redlands High School, Redlands, CA**

CORN CHIP CHILI

Serves 8 - 10   **MEXICO**

1 1/2 cups onion, chopped
1 tablespoon vegetable oil
1 clove garlic
1 1/2 pounds ground beef
3 (16 ounce) cans black or red beans,
    drained
1 (20 ounce) can enchilada sauce

2 cups cheddar cheese, grated
1 1/2 tablespoon chili powder
4 - 6 cups tortilla or corn chips
1 cup plain yogurt or sour cream
1 tablespoon cilantro, chopped finely
1/2 teaspoon cumin

Brown onions in oil for 3 minutes. Add garlic and beef and cook until meat is browned; drain off fat. Add drained beans, enchilada sauce, cheese, chili powder and stir well. Arrange chips in a greased 3 quart casserole and top with meat and bean mixture. Bake at 350 degrees for 30 minutes. Meanwhile, mix yogurt with cilantro and cumin. When ready to serve, pass this sauce to spoon over corn chip chili.

"At a picnic or as a fundraiser, you can cut small bags of corn chips in half (with the corn chips left equally in each half) and spoon on the chili mixture. This makes an easily carried serving of corn chip chili to be eaten on the move with plastic utensil."

Larkin Evans   **Half Moon Bay High School, Half Moon Bay, CA**

CHILI QUITAS

Serves 4

1/2 pound ground pork or 2 pork chops, diced
4 cloves garlic, minced
1/3 cup vinegar
3 cups water
1 (8 ounce) can tomato sauce + 2 cans water

1 (12 ounce) bottle Ortega mild green chili salsa
1 (4 ounce) can Ortega green chiles, diced
tortilla chips
Monterey jack cheese, grated

Brown ground pork or pork chops and garlic. Drain. Add vinegar and water; simmer 10 minutes in covered pan. Add tomato sauce plus 2 cans of water, salsa and chilies. Simmer 15 minutes longer in covered pan. Pour sauce over chips and sprinkle with grated cheese.

"This is a quick dinner to fix!"

Ginger Russo **Chico Junior High School, Chico, CA**

BISQUICK ONE PAN MEXICAN STYLE BEEF BAKE

Serves 6 **MEXICO**

1 pound ground beef, cooked and drained
2 cups Bisquick baking mix
2/3 cup milk
2 eggs
1/2 cup onion, chopped

1 to 2 tablespoons chili powder
1/2 teaspoon ground cumin
1/2 teaspoon garlic powder
1 cup cheddar cheese, shredded
2 tomatoes, chopped

Brown ground beef and cook until done; drain off fat; set aside. Mix baking mix, milk and eggs in greased 11" x 7" x 1/2" pan with fork until uniform in color (batter will be lumpy). Stir in cooked beef, onion and seasonings; spread evenly. Bake at 350 degrees, uncovered until top springs back when touched lightly in center, 25 to 30 minutes. Sprinkle with cheese and tomatoes. Bake just until cheese is melted, 1 - 2 minutes longer. Serve with taco sauce, sour cream or guacamole if desired.

"My friend Grace Meza, our school secretary, gave me this recipe. It's quick and easy to prepare."

Darlene Brown **Golden Valley Middle School, San Bernardino, CA**

BURRITO PIE

Serves 6 **MEXICO**

4 (8 inch) flour tortillas
1/4 cup salad oil
1/2 pound ground beef
1 medium onion, diced
1 small garlic clove, minced
1 (4 ounce) can chopped green chilies, drained
1 (8 ounce) can refried beans

1/3 cup hot taco sauce
salt, to taste
1/2 pound jack cheese, shredded (about 2 cups)
1 cup lettuce, shredded
1 medium tomato, diced
5 large pitted ripe olives, sliced

About 1 hour before serving: In a 10 inch skillet over medium heat, fry 1 tortilla at a time in salad oil, about 30 seconds on each side or until lightly browned and blistered. Remove to paper towels to drain. Discard any remaining oil. Preheat oven to 350 degrees. In same skillet, over high heat, cook ground beef, onion and garlic until all pan juices evaporate and meat is well browned. Remove from heat and stir in green chilies, refried beans, taco sauce and salt. In a 9" pie plate, place 1 tortilla, top with 1/4 of beef-bean mixture and 1/4 of cheese. Repeat three times. Bake pie 30 minutes or until heated through. Sprinkle pie with shredded lettuce, diced tomato and olives.

Judi Topp   **A.B.Miller High School, Fontana, CA**

FESTIVE TAMALE PIE

Serves 8   **MEXICO**

1 cup onion, chopped
1 cup bell pepper, chopped
1 pound ground beef or turkey
1/2 pound sausage
2 (8 ounce) cans tomato sauce
1 (12 ounce) can whole kernel corn, drained
1 cup ripe olives, chopped
1 clove garlic, minced

1 tablespoon sugar
dash pepper
2 teaspoons chili powder
1 1/2 cups cheddar cheese, shredded
3/4 cup yellow cornmeal
1/2 teaspoon salt
2 cups cold water
1 tablespoon butter or margarine

Cook onion and bell pepper in pan sprayed with non-stick cooking spray until tender. Add meat and brown lightly. Add tomato sauce, corn, olives, garlic, sugar, pepper and chili powder. Simmer 20 minutes or until thick. Add cheese and stir until melted. Pour into 9" x 13" pan coated with non-stick cooking spray. Stir cornmeal and salt into cold water. Cook and stir until thick. Add butter or margarine and mix well. Spread over meat mixture and bake at 350 degrees for 40 minutes.

Donna Swennes   **El Capitan High School, Lakeside, CA**

QUICK CRESCENT TACO PIE

Serves 4 - 6   **MEXICO**

1 1/4 pound ground beef
1 package taco seasoning
1/2 cup water
1/2 cup olives, sliced
1 can crescent rolls

1 1/2 - 2 cups corn chips, crushed
1 cup sour cream
1 cup cheddar cheese, grated
lettuce, shredded

In large fry pan, brown ground beef; drain. Stir in seasoning mix, water and olives. Simmer 5 minutes. Meanwhile, separate crescent rolls into 8 triangles. Place triangles in an ungreased 9" to 10" pie pan, pressing to form a crust. Sprinkle 1 cup of corn chips over bottom of crust. Spoon meat mixture over chips. Spread sour cream over meat mixture; cover with cheese. Sprinkle on remaining corn chips. Bake at 375 degrees for 20 to 25 minutes. Remove from oven and sprinkle with shredded lettuce before serving.

"Easy and yummy."

Robin Ali-Christie   **Nevada Union High School, Grass Valley, CA**

TIJUANA TORTE

Serves 4 - 6   **MEXICO**

1 pound ground beef
1 medium onion, chopped
1 (1 pound) can stewed tomatoes
1 (8 ounce) can tomato sauce

1 (4 ounce) can green chilies, chopped
1 package taco seasoning mix
12 corn tortillas
1 pound cheddar cheese, grated

Brown the ground beef and onion in a skillet. Drain off fat. Add stewed tomatoes, tomato sauce, green chilies and taco mix. Combine thoroughly and simmer 10 to 15 minutes. Place about 1/4 cup of the meat mixture in the bottom of a 9" x 13" baking dish. Place 2 tortillas side by side on the meat mixture. Top each tortilla with some meat mixture and grated cheese. Repeat until each stack contains 6 tortillas layered with meat and cheese. Bake at 350 degrees for 20 to 25 minutes, until cheese is bubbly. Cut each stack into quarters with a sharp knife before serving.

"This is a recipe I got from Lawry Foods. My students have enjoyed making and eating it."

Amber Bradley   **Granite Hills High School, El Cajon, CA**

CHICKEN CHALUPAS

Serves 10 - 12   **MEXICO**

1 (2 pound) chicken
1 small onion
1 clove garlic
1 pint sour cream
salt, to taste
16 - 18 corn tortillas

oil for frying
1/2 green pepper, diced
1 can roasted green chilies, diced
1 pound cheddar cheese, grated
1/4 teaspoon paprika

Boil chicken until tender, reserving some broth. Remove bones and cut into bite-sized pieces. Grate onion and garlic into sour cream. Add salt and some broth to thin sour cream. Soften tortillas by dipping in hot oil and drain on paper towels. Fill each tortilla with chicken, peppers, chilies and cheese (reserving 1 cup cheese for topping), place in a flat pan, seam side down. Pour sour cream mixture over top, sprinkle remaining cheese and paprika on top and refrigerate for 8 hours. Bake at 350 degrees for 1 hour.(This can also be frozen and baked later - thaw before baking.)

"This is a recipe I got from my mother. It's good to fix ahead or freeze for later."

Anita Huckert   **Greenfield Junior High School, Bakersfield, CA**

CHICKEN QUESADILLAS

Serves 4   MEXICO

1 can cream of chicken soup
1 1/2 cup cooked chicken, chopped
1 cup cheddar cheese, shredded, divided

8 flour tortillas (8 inches each)
salsa, to serve
sour cream, to serve

In a small bowl, combine soup, chicken and 1/2 cup cheddar cheese. Top half of each tortilla with 1/4 cup soup mixture, spreading evenly to within 1/2 inch of edge. Moisten edges of tortillas with water; fold over, pressing edges to seal. Arrange filled tortillas on two large baking sheets. Bake at 400 degrees for 8 minutes. Remove from oven and sprinkle with remaining 1/2 cup cheese. Serve with salsa and sour cream.

Jeanette Atkinson   **Brinley Middle School, Las Vegas, NV**

MONSTER BURRITO MIX

Serves 4 - 8   MEXICO

1 pound lean hamburger
1 medium yellow onion, finely chopped
1 cup salsa (you pick heat)

1 (30 ounce) can refried beans
12 - 18 medium-sized flour tortillas
2 cups cheddar cheese, grated

Brown hamburger; add onion and simmer 5 minutes. Add salsa and beans; simmer 10 minutes. Warm tortillas. Put 3 tablespoons filling in each tortilla; top with cheese and fold up.

"Quick and easy Mexican style main dish for midday or evening meals."

Will Scarrow   **Marshall Middle School, Long Beach, CA**

STIR-FRIED PORK BURRITOS

Serves 4   MEXICO

1 pound lean boneless pork loin
2 cloves garlic, minced
1 teaspoon oregano, crumbled
1 teaspoon ground cumin
1 teaspoon seasoned salt
2 tablespoons orange juice

2 tablespoons vinegar
1/2 teaspoon hot pepper sauce, or to taste
1 tablespoon vegetable oil
1 medium onion, peeled and sliced
1 green pepper, seeded and sliced
4 flour tortillas

Slice pork across grain grain into 1/8" strips. Mix together garlic, oregano, cumin, salt, orange juice, vinegar and hot pepper sauce. Marinate pork strips in mixture for 10 minutes. Heat oil in heavy skillet or on griddle until hot. Stir-fry pork strips, onion and green pepper until pork is no longer pink, about 3 - 5 minutes. Serve with flour tortillas and accompany with sliced green onion, shredded lettuce and salsa, if desired.

National Pork Producers Council   **Des Moines, IA**

CHICKEN ENCHILADAS

Serves 6   MEXICO

1 1/2 chicken breasts
3 tablespoons oil
1/2 cup flour
1 (28 ounce) can red chili sauce
1 teaspoon sugar
salt, to taste
ground chili powder, to taste

1 pint sour cream
1 cup Monterey jack cheese, shredded
1 cup cheddar cheese, shredded
12 corn tortillas
1 (2 1/4 ounce) can black olives, sliced
1 large onion, finely chopped
green onions, chopped (optional)

Cook chicken in water to cover until tender, cool and discard skin and bones; finely shred meat. Reserve broth. Heat oil in large saucepan. Add flour and stir 1 minute. Stir in red chili sauce and half a chili sauce can of reserved chicken broth. Add sugar; season to taste with salt and chili powder. Add sour cream; blend well. Add 1/2 cup each jack and cheddar cheese and let melt. To assemble enchiladas, fry each tortilla in oil until softened; drain. In each tortilla, place some of the chicken, olives, onion and a little cheese plus a tablespoon of sauce. Roll and place seam side down in individual, heat-proof plates, pie plates or 13" x 9" baking dish. Top with sauce, using at least 2 cups, more if desired. Sprinkle with remaining shredded cheeses. Bake at 350 degrees until cheese melts and sauce is bubbly. Top with green onions.

NOTE: Remaining sauce can be frozen for another batch of enchiladas.

Pam Ford   **Temecula Valley High School, Temecula, CA**

CHICKEN ENCHILADAS

Serves 6   MEXICO

6 whole chicken breasts, cut in half
1 cup onion, chopped
2 tablespoons margarine
1 (16 ounce) can whole tomatoes, cut up
1 (8 ounce) chunky Ortega green
   chili salsa
1 teaspoon sugar
1 teaspoon ground cumin

1/2 teaspoon salt
1/2 teaspoon whole leaf oregano
1/2 teaspoon basil
1 dozen flour tortillas, taco size
8 ounces jack cheese, cut into
   3/4" x 3/4" x 4"
3/4 cup sour cream
1 cup cheddar cheese, grated

Precook chicken; cool, debone and remove skin; cut into 12 pieces. Prepare sauce by sauteeing onion in margarine, stir in tomatoes, salsa and seasonings; simmer 10 minutes. To assemble enchiladas, soften tortilla in sauce; place a piece of chicken and a stick of jack cheese in center and fold over. Place seam side down in a 13" x 9" x 2" pan. Repeat with remaining tortillas. Stir sour cream into remaining sauce. Pour over enchiladas. Top with grated cheese. Bake at 350 degrees for 40 minutes.

"Easy and soooo good, a family favorite. I serve with Spanish rice and a green salad with orange sections and toasted almonds."

Lorna Wilfert   **Huntington Beach High School, Huntington Beach, CA**

FLAT CHEESE ENCHILADAS

Serves 4 - 6   **MEXICO**

1/4 cup salad oil   2 cups ground beef, cooked
12 corn tortillas   1 small onion, minced
1 large can Las Palmas enchilada sauce   2 cups jack cheese, grated

Heat oil in a skillet and soften tortillas one at a time. Drain each tortilla as you remove it
from the skillet. Put some enchilada sauce on a large Pyrex dish, then take a softened tortilla
and place it into the sauce. Add ground beef, then onion and cheese. Repeat until you use
up all the ingredients, stacking tortillas. Cut into 4 or 6 parts, heat in hot oven (375 degrees)
for 5 minutes to melt cheese.

*"You can make this dish ahead of time and store in the refrigerator overnight. For
variety, use other cooked meats such as chicken, pork or crab (canned or fresh).
Along the Texas/Mexican border, enchiladas are not rolled up. They are served
flat and stacked."*

Mary Katen   **Central Valley High School, Central Valley, CA**

GUADALAJARA TACOS

Makes 1 dozen   **MEXICO**

1 pound ground or shredded beef   6 large black olives, pitted and sliced
1 package taco mix   6 pepperoni, sliced and quartered
2 medium apples, cored, peeled, diced   lettuce
2/3 (9 ounce) box raisins, whole or   tomatoes, chopped
   chopped   cheese, grated
1/2 cup dry roasted peanuts, whole   12 tortillas, hard or soft, as desired
   or halved   salsa

In a skillet, brown the ground beef. Drain off fat. Add the taco mix and amount of water
instructed on package. Add next 5 ingredients; stir. Simmer for at least 45 minutes. Serve
with lettuce, chopped tomatoes and grated cheese on hard or soft taco shells. Add salsa
if desired.

*"This recipe was created by a Mexican chef in Guadalajara, Mexico. I love it
because it is so different and tasty."*

Vicki Agee   **San Marcos High School, San Marcos, CA**

TAQUITOS AL PASTOR

Serves 12   **MEXICO**

3 pounds boneless pork shoulder   1 1/2 cups white vinegar
8 dried red chilies, seeded and crushed   1/2 teaspoon oregano
1/2 cup vegetable oil   salt and pepper to taste
1 1/4 cups pineapple juice   2 cups pineapple cubes
4 cloves garlic, peeled   1 bunch fresh cilantro, chopped
1 tablespoon chicken bouillon granules   24 fresh corn or flour tortillas

Blend together chilies, oil, pineapple juice, garlic, chicken bouillon, vinegar, oregano, salt and pepper in blender until smooth. Simmer in saucepan 15 minutes. Marinate pork in mixture 4 - 12 hours; refrigerated. Discard marinade. Roast pork, covered, with pineapple cubes for 2 hours at 350 degrees. Cool slightly and shred pork; serve with onion, cilantro and tortillas.

National Pork Producers Council   **Des Moines, IA**

MEXICAN COCOA TORTE

Serves 8 - 10   **MEXICO**

1 cup sugar   *1/4 teaspoon ground cinnamon*
1/2 cup Hershey's Cocoa   *1 (11 ounce) package pie crust mix*
1/2 cup strong coffee   *2 cups cold whipping cream*
1/3 cup shortening   *Hershey's Mini-Chips, semi-sweet chocolate*

In small saucepan, combine sugar, cocoa, coffee, shortening and cinnamon. Cook over very low heat, stirring constantly until smooth and creamy. Cool to room temperature. Stir together pie crust mix and 3/4 cup of the cocoa mixture, blending well. Shape into smooth ball; refrigerate 1 hour. Heat oven to 350 degrees. Line two cookie sheets with foil; mark two 8" circles on each. Cut pastry ball into 4 pieces; form each into small ball. Place balls of pastry on foil; press with fingers into marked circles. Bake 10 to 12 minutes or until almost set; cool on cookie sheets. In small mixer bowl, combine whipping cream and remaining cocoa mixture; beat until stiff. Place one pastry round on serving plate; spread with one-fourth whipped cream mixture. Repeat layering with remaining three rounds and whipped cream mixture, ending with whipped cream. Refrigerate several hours; cut in wedges to serve. Garnish with small chocolate chips.

Hershey Foods Corp.   **Hershey, PA**

FLAN

Serves 8 - 10   **MEXICO**

6 eggs   *1 (3 ounce) package cream cheese*
1 (12 ounce) can evaporated milk   *1/2 teaspoon vanilla*
1 (14 ounce) can sweetened   *cinnamon, to taste*
  condensed milk   *1/2 cup sugar*

Blend first six ingredients in blender until foamy; about 1 minute. Set aside. Melt sugar in saucepan until golden brown. Pour into casserole (2 quart) dish and swirl quickly. Pour egg mixture on top. Bake, uncovered, in a water bath at 350 degrees for 1 hour or until set. Invert onto serving platter. Serve warm or chilled.

"My sister-in-law, Emilia, who lives in Mexico City, prepared this for my family and it's been a family favorite ever since."

Diane Lizardi   **Downey High School, Downey, CA**

Tortilla Roll-Ups, Page 110

Mexican Cocoa Torte, Page 124

Hot & Spicy Beef Ribs, Page 14

Apple Nut Lattice Tart, Page 20

MIDDLE EAST

Israel
Lebanon
Mediterranean
Saudi Arabia

It is hard to identify "Middle Eastern" food and claim one dish as strictly Egyptian, Lebanese, Jewish, Arabic, or Turkish. Many of the same recipes turn up in several Middle Eastern countries.

The early origin of Middle Eastern food goes back to those peoples who ruled the region and held the strongest influence over the society. There were the Persians, whose love of good food and lavish banquets perpetuated the glories for their predecessors, the Greeks and Romans.

There was also the pharaoic influences of Egypt, with recipes including roast goose, melokhia soup, bamia and betareck (Egyptian vegetable dishes).

The peasantry of each region probably was the most influential force in Middle Eastern cooking, although they possessed a limited variety of foods. The Bedouin tradition included milk, lamb, and dates...the food of the desert and oasis.

In more recent history, the Middle East has become more cosmopolitan. Today, the renowned restaurants of the Middle East offer a double menu: traditional and cosmopolitan.

Middle East

MRS. RICHMOND´S HUMMUS RECIPE

Serves many   **MIDDLE EAST**

2 (15 ounce) cans garbanzo beans   1/4 teaspoon cumin
1/3 cup fresh lemon juice   3 shakes seasoned salt
1/2 cup tahini oil (ground sesame seeds) 3 shakes paprika
3 cloves garlic, crushed   1 tablespoon olive oil
1 tablespoon fresh mint, or Italian parsley   parsley, as a garnish

Drain liquid from garbanzo beans, reserving 1/4 cup liquid. Place liquid and lemon juice
in blender; add beans and puree, scraping the sides of the container often. Transfer to bowl
and stir in tahini, garlic, mint, cumin, seasoned salt, paprika and olive oil. Refrigerate,
covered, for at least 6 hours (overnight is best). Pour the dip into a shallow bowl, make a
well in center and add another 3-4 tablespoons olive oil. Garnish with chopped parsley, a
shake of paprika and olives, if desired. Serve with wedges of pita bread, or carrot and celery
sticks.

NOTE: Can be stored in refrigerator up to 2 weeks.

*"In the United States, hummus is sometimes called a garbanzo bean and garlic
dip...but in the Middle East, it is called Hummus Bi Tahini. It is served in Turkey
at a meze or appetizer course with many different kinds of dips, spreads, salads,
etc."*

Mary Richmond   **San Luis Obispo High School, San Luis Obispo, CA**

SPINACH PIES

Serves 10 - 20   **LEBANON**

2 packages refrigerated biscuits   1/2 teaspoon allspice
2 packages frozen spinach, chopped   2 1/2 teaspoons cumin
1 medium onion, chopped   1 1/2 tablespoons lemon juice
1/2 green pepper, chopped   2 teaspoons oil
1/2 teaspoon salt

Bring biscuit dough to room temperature. Thaw spinach in microwave and drain to remove
all liquid. Remove biscuits from packages and roll out into 4 inch circles. Mix thoroughly
drained spinach with chopped onion and green pepper. Add seasonings. Mix in lemon juice
and oil. Place one heaping spoonful of spinach mixture on each biscuit round. Fold round
in half. Pinch edges to seal. Place on ungreased cookie sheet. Brush tops with oil. Bake at
350 degrees for 25 to 30 minutes.

"This recipe is quick, easy and delicious. Always a hit at buffets."

Adrienne Pringle   **Royal High School, Simi Valley, CA**

CHICK PEA DIP

Serves 8 - 10   LEBANON

1 (15 ounce) can chick peas, drained   *1/2 teaspoon salt*
   reserving liquid & 10 peas for garnish   *1/4 cup reserved liquid (from tahini)*
1/4 cup tahini, prepared as directed below   *parsley for garnish*
3 tablespoons fresh lemon juice   *paprika for garnish*
2 medium garlic cloves

First, mix the tahini as follows: When you open the can or jar of tahini, you will find liquid on top (like natural peanut butter - oil rises to the top). Pour the liquid into a blender then take one spoonful of tahini residue and add it to the liquid, blending at high speed. Repeat until the whole can or jar is mixed. Return mixture to can or jar. (Do not try to put it all in at once, as it can be too much for the blender's motor and cause damage.)

Put chick peas (reserving 10 for garnish) and remaining ingredients in blender and blend at high speed until smooth. Pour dip into a serving dish. Place the whole peas in the middle, garish with parsley and sprinkle with paprika. Serve with Pita bread, cut into wedges.

Ruth Anne Mills   **Los Alisos Intermediate School, Mission Viejo, CA**

ARAB BREAD

Makes 8 loaves   **SAUDI ARABIA**

2 packages active dry yeast   *2 teaspoons salt*
pinch of sugar   *1/4 cup olive oil*
3 cups lukewarm water, divided   *1/2 cup cornmeal*
7 - 8 cups flour

In glass measuring cup, dissolve yeast and sugar in 1/2 cup lukewarm water. Let stand in a warm place for 10 minutes. Place 6 cups flour on a pastry board and make a 12" well in the center. Pour in salt, olive oil, and remaining 2 1/2 cups lukewarm water. Add yeast. Carefully work flour into liquid mixture, using just enough flour to form dough into a ball. You might not use all of the flour, or you may add more, but do not make the dough too stiff. Knead dough for 20 minutes on a lightly floured surface, until smooth and elastic. Add more flour only to keep dough from sticking to the board. Shape dough into a ball, placing in a lightly oiled bowl. Cover and let rise until dough is double in bulk. Punch down and divide into 8 equal pieces. Knead each piece into smooth balls. Cover with towel and allow to rise for 30 minutes. Sprinkle 2 baking sheets with cornmeal. On a lightly floured surface, roll 4 balls of dough into 8" round loaves, 1/8" thick. Place 2 loaves on each baking sheet 2" to 3" apart. Cover and allow to rest for 30 minutes. Preheat oven to 500 degrees. Bake on bottom oven rack for 3 minutes or until loaves puff up. Transfer to oven rack 3" to 4" higher and continue baking for 3 minutes or until light brown. Remove from oven and wrap each loaf in foil, making it airtight. Set aside for 10 minutes. Continue for remaining balls of dough. When loaves are unwrapped, they will have fallen, making a pocket of air in the center. Serve warm or at room temperature.

"This recipe requires a large block of time to make, but it is worth the effort."
Cathy Miller   **Montclair High School, Montclair, CA**

JEWISH PENICILLIN (CHICKEN SOUP)

Serves 6 - 8   **ISRAEL**

1 (4 - 5 pounds) chicken
4 stalks celery, chopped
1 large onion, diced
4 carrots, peeled, sliced
1 bunch parsnips, diced
1 celery root, diced

1 bunch parsleyroot, chopped
handful parsley, chopped
handful dill, chopped
water to cover amply (at least 4 - 5
*   quarts)*
salt and pepper, to taste

Put all ingredients into pot with water and cover. Bring to boil; let simmer for 2 hours, until everything is tender and soft. As the soup simmers, skim off bubbly foam. After two hours, remove chicken and cut into small pieces. If you wish, take out all vegetables and mash or puree. Add back to broth along with chicken. Add salt and pepper to taste.

"Rabbi Jackie was a guest demonstrator/speaker on the Jewish food habits and traditions in my Foods & Nutrition classes. This recipe is the real thing - guaranteed to make you well!"

Barbara Hansen   **Montclair High School, Montclair, CA**

ETHNIC POTATO SALAD

Serves 6   **MIDDLE EAST**

3 medium white potatoes, cooked
2 sweet potatoes, cooked
3/4 cup celery, chopped
1/2 cup green onion, chopped
3 eggs, hardboiled and chopped

curry powder, to taste
salt, to taste
pepper to taste
3/4 cup mayonnaise

Peel and dice potatoes. Mix in celery, onion and eggs. Mix curry powder, salt, pepper and mayonnaise to taste. Blend dressing and salad. Refrigerate overnight to blend flavors.

"This is a great post-Thanksgiving dish. Put in a bit of the turkey and chop up the leftover deviled eggs."

Lynda Ruth   **La Mirada High School, La Mirada, CA**

TABBOULI SALAD

Serves 10 - 12   **MIDDLE EAST**

1 cup fine bulga
1/4 cup hot water
1 large head Romaine lettuce
1 1/2 cups green onion, chopped
*   (include tops)*
1 1/2 cups parsley, chopped

1 1/2 cups fresh mint leaves, chopped
1/2 cup oil (preferably olive oil)
1/3 cup lemon juice
2 teaspoons salt
2 ripe tomatoes

Wash the bulgar 2 to 3 times in water; drain. In a large container, pour hot water on the bulgar and let it stand about 1/2 hour or until lightly puffed. (Bulgar will almost double in size.) Wash all greens well and dry; chop. In a jar with tight fitting lid, mix oil, lemon juice and salt. Shake the mixture well so the salt will dissolve. To assemble: mix all greens, tomatoes and bulgar in a large container so mixing will be easy. Mix well. Add oil dressing only just before serving and toss well.

"This recipe is a favorite salad in the San Joaquin Valley."

Nancy Jordan   **Merced High School, Merced, CA**

MEDITERRANEAN VEGETABLES

Serves 4   **MEDITERRANEAN**

1 (6 ounce) jar marinated artichoke
   hearts, drained (reserve marinade)
1 medium carrot
1 1/2 cups broccoli, chopped
1 medium red bell pepper, chopped
1 medium yellow bell pepper, chopped
3 medium pear tomatoes, sliced

1 tablespoon oregano
1/2 cup Calamata olives, pitted and
   quartered
2 tablespoons capers, drained and
   minced
4 ounces feta cheese, crumbled
1 lemon, cut into quarters

Drain the artichokes, reserving 3 tablespoons marinade. Cut them into halves or quarters, depending on their size. Set aside. In a wok or stir-fry pan, heat the reserved marinade over medium heat. Add the carrot and broccoli, cooking 5 minutes, stirring occasionally. Add the peppers, tomatoes and oregano, then cook for 10 minutes. Toss the vegetables occasionally so they cook evenly. Stir in the olives, capers and artichokes and heat through. Serve with feta cheese and a lemon wedge for each serving.

"I tried this recipe from a vegetarian cookbook I bought at my son's college bookstore. I really liked the lemon flavor."

Linda Robinson   **Royal High School, Simi Valley, CA**

RICE PILAF

Serves 4 - 6   **MIDDLE EAST**

4 - 6 tablespoons butter or margarine
1/2 cup vermicelli or 2 coils vermicelli
1 cup long grain rice

2 cups chicken broth
salt and pepper to taste

Melt the butter in a 2 quart saucepan. Break up vermicelli into pieces and fry in butter until slightly browned, stirring constantly. Add rice to the vermicelli and saute them together for a few minutes, stirring constantly. In another saucepan, bring chicken broth to a boil and add to rice mixture. Season with salt and pepper; cover and cook on low heat for 20 minutes. When water is all absorbed and rice is soft, take off stove and let rest for 15 to 20 minutes before serving. Stir once more with a fork. Serve hot.

Olga Sarouhan   **Edison High School, Huntington Beach, CA**

MEDITERRANEAN PASTA

Serves 4

8 slices bacon, coarsely chopped
3 cloves garlic, minced
1 pound escarole, or 1 (10 ounce)
   package frozen chopped spinach
1 (16 ounce) can whole tomatoes, in
   juice, undrained, coarsely chopped

1/2 teaspoon salt (optional)
1/8 - 1/4 teaspoon crushed red pepper
1/2 cup ripe olives, pitted and sliced
6 ounces mostaccioli, cooked and
drained

In a large skillet, cook bacon until crisp. Remove all but 1 tablespoon drippings. Add garlic; saute 30 seconds. Add escarole, cook 3 minutes or until wilted. Add tomatoes, salt and crushed red pepper, stirring occasionally. Cook 5 minutes. Add olives, cook 3 minutes. Toss with mostaccioli.

Note: try substituting 1 package frozen artichoke hearts for the escarole. Yummy!!!

"Oh! SO yummy!"

Sheryal Walther　　　　　　　　　　**Lakewood High School, Lakewood, CA**

TURKEY DUMPLINGS

Serves 6

1 pound California- grown ground turkey
2/3 cup tabbouleh*
1/3 cup parsley, chopped
2 tablespoons fresh mint, chopped
   OR 1 teaspoon dried mint
1 teaspoon paprika

1/4 teaspoon cinnamon
salt & cayenne pepper to taste
3 (14 1/2 ounces each) cans beef broth
1 1/2 cups water
3 tablespoons tomato paste
1/2 cup plain yogurt

Knead turkey with tabbouleh, spices and seasonings, reserving 1 tablespoon parsley. Form into 12 balls and chill. Combine beef broth, water and tomato paste and bring to a boil. Drop the dumplings in boiling broth about six at a time; cook five minutes. Remove with slotted spoon; cook remaining dumplings. Serve dumplings in broth garnished with dollop of yogurt and sprinkle with parsley.

*Prepare 1 (7 ounce) box Tabbouleh Salad Mix without tomato; retain unused portion for other use.

California Poultry Industry Federation　　　　　　　　　**Modesto, CA**

FALAFEL TURKEY BUNDT LOAF

Serves 8 - 10

2 eggs
1/2 cups water
2/3 cup tomato and basil sauce
1 (6 ounce) package Falafel Mix

2 pounds ground turkey
1 clove garlic, pressed
1 teaspoon ginger, minced

6 ounces garbanzo beans, drained
1/2 cup light sour cream

Beat eggs with a fork. Add water and tomato sauce and continue beating. Stir in falafel mix; let stand 5 minutes. Add ground turkey, garlic and ginger; mix thoroughly. Spread evenly into a bundt pan. Bake at 350 degrees for 60 minutes.

Sauce: In a blender, blend cucumber, dill, garbanzo beans and sour cream until smooth. Refrigerate sauce until ready to use.

"Chunk leftovers, cut up cucumber and tomato and serve in pita bread with the sauce."

Becky Oppen   **Dana Hills High School, Dana Point, CA**

ZUCCHINI EGGAH WITH TOMATO GARNISH

Serves 4 - 6   **MIDDLE EAST**

4 tablespoons virgin olive oil
1 cup scallions, thinly sliced or chopped
1 cup fresh parsley, chopped
1/4 tesapoon freshly ground pepper
1 tesapoon ground cumin
1 toaspoon ground coriander

4 cups zucchini, shredded
    (2 - 3 medium)
1 1/2 teaspoons salt
Zest from 1/2 lemon, grated
6 eggs, lightly beaten

Garnish:
6 medium red tomatoes, coarsley chopped, juices reserved
1 generous dash hot pepper sauce
1/2 cup fresh dill, cut in 1/8 inch lengths

In a heavy skillet, heat the oil over medium heat. Add the scallions, parsley, pepper, cumin and coriander. Saute for 3 minutes. Add the zucchini, salt and lemon zest and stir until zucchini heats through and begins to wilt. Reduce heat to low. Pour the eggs over the zucchini mixture and stir to mix. Level the mixture; cover with a tight-fitting lid and cook the eggah slowly for about 10 minutes, or until eggs are set. Check the eggah now and then to make sure it is not burning and adjust the burner if necessary.

While the eggah is cooking, toss the tomatoes with their juices, the hot pepper sauce and snipped dill; set aside. For best flavor, do not refrigerate the garnish. When the eggah is done, cut into wedges and top each wedge with tomato garnish. Serve with French bread and a leafy salad.

"This is a truly delightful Middle-Eastern recipe I found this summer."

Sheryal Walther   **Lakewood High School, Lakewood, CA**

SCANDINAVIA

Denmark
Holland
Finland
Norway
Sweden

The countries that make up the region known as Scandinavia have traditionally been associated with the Viking heritage. This is true enough, but it is not the only historical nor culinary influence. The foods and customs of Scandinavia are intermingled along with the different countries that make up this region.

Through the ages, Scandinavian diets have varied, but they are always down to earth. Delectable fish, from the abundant waters of the North see to that, but pork and poultry can be found on the menu, too.

The foods of Scandinavia reflect the physical characteristics of the region. They smack of the sea, or of a freshwater lake, or even the earth.

SCANDINAVIA

SWEDISH MEATBALLS

Serves 8 - 10   **SWEDEN**

1 1/2 pound ground beef
1/2 pound pork sausage
1 cup seasoned bread crumbs
1 onion, minced
1 cup milk
2 eggs

1/2 teaspoon salt
dash of pepper
2 cups packed brown sugar
6 tablespoons vinegar
2 teaspoons dry mustard

Combine first 8 ingredients in bowl; mix well. Shape into small balls. Place in baking pan.
Refrigerate overnight. Bring brown sugar, vinegar and dry mustard to a boil in saucepan.
Boil for 1 minute. Pour over meatballs. Bake at 350 degrees for 1 hour. Serve on warming
plate with toothpicks.

Penny Childers   **Ramona High School, Ramona, CA**

DANISH EBLESKIVERS

Makes 75 to 80   **DENMARK**

6 eggs, separated
2 cups buttermilk
2 cups flour
2 tablespoons sugar
1 teaspoon baking soda

1/2 teaspoon salt
oil for frying
powdered sugar

Beat whites until stiff peaks form. Beat egg yolks until thick and lemon-colored. Mix
buttermilk, flour, sugar, baking soda and salt into egg yolk. Gently fold in egg whites. Place
a small amount of oil into each cup of an ebleskiver pan. Heat pan over medium heat. Fill
each cup 2/3 full. Cook until bubbly and set around edges. Turn with toothpick. Cook on
other side. Remove from pan and serve warm, dusted with powdered sugar.

"My family loves them, and my students have a great time making them."

Kristine Haas   **La Habra High School, La Habra, CA**

NISUA (FINNISH COFFEE CAKE)

Serves 12+   FINLAND

4 eggs
1 cup sugar
2 cups scalded milk
1/2 cup margarine, melted

8 cups flour
1 teaspoon cardamom seed, crushed
2 packages dry yeast

Beat eggs; add scalded milk and sugar. Beat in 3 cups flour, yeast and cardamom. Add 2 more cups flour. Beat in melted margarine. Beat in 3 more cups flour. Let rise until double in size. Punch down. Divide dough into 9 parts. Roll each part into a long sheet and braid together, 3 pieces at a time (makes 3 loaves). Let rise again. Bake in preheated oven at 375 degrees for 10 minutes or 325 degrees for 15 to 20 minutes. After "Nisua" has baked for 10 minutes, remove from oven and brush with milk and sprinkle with sugar. Return to oven to finish baking.

"This recipe was given to me by my mother-in-law. Her parents were from Finland and she is a terrific cook of many Finnish goodies like this coffee cake."

Sandra Robertson   **Whittier High School, Whittier, CA**

LEFSE

Serves 30   SCANDINAVIA

5 pounds cooked potatoes, riced
   or mashed
1/2 cup butter, melted
1 tablespoon cream

salt to taste
3 cups flour
3 1/2 teaspoons sugar

When potatoes are done cooking, set aside to cool. When cooled, add butter, cream and salt to taste. Combine flour and sugar and add to potato mixture. Mixture will be heavy. Cut off small balls of dough to roll out as you proceed making the potato "tortillas". Roll each ball of dough thin with a "knobby" rolling pin, which will give the lefsa "bumps". (Be sure to use enough flour so the lefsa doesn't stick to the pastry cloth.) Using a lefsa stick (a long, flat stick to turn lefsa when baking), slide the stick under the center of the round "tortilla" and place on a hot grill. (No oil is necessary, but a small amount of non-stick spray may be used.) Bake on both sides of lefsa until "bumps" are brown. After cooling, but still warm, spread with butter and sprinkle with sugar for a dessert treat OR fill with potatoes, gravy and meat and fold like a burritos. It is traditionally served with lutafisk, a type of salted fish. Store in an airtight container in refrigerator up to a week or freeze. Our family likes to eat it as it is being made, still warm and very fresh!

"This has been a treat I have enjoyed since my childhood and visit to Grandma's would always mean something special when she was making fresh lefsa. The tradition has been handed down to my mother and now to me. My boys enjoy lefsa, and I hope they will learn how to make it some day too!"

Barbara Allen   **Ayala High School, Chino, CA**

LEFSE

Makes 20

4 cups mashed potatoes
2 cups flour

scant 1/4 cup shortening
1 tablespoon salt

Combine all ingredients and form into 2 inch balls. Roll out like pie crust and bake on a dry (no oil) griddle like you would do a pancake on medium-high heat for 2 to 3 minutes each. (You might want to brush off the excess flour from rolling it out before placing on griddle.)

"When we made a cookbook in the 4th grade, my teacher entitled my contribution Mary calls this Lefse"

Mary Cronkhite   **Antelope Valley High School, Lancaster, CA**

OLE´S SWEDISH HOTCAKES

Serves 4

1 cup flour
1 teaspoon sugar
1/4 teaspoon salt
1 teaspoon baking powder

1 1/2 cups milk
1/2 cup half and half
3 eggs
3/4 cup (6 tablespoons) butter, melted

Mix the dry ingredients together. Add the milk and half and half and mix thoroughly. Separate whites of eggs and beat until stiff. Beat egg yolks and add to batter. Fold in egg whites, then the butter. Cook on a hot, lightly greased, griddle. Serve with butter and syrup.

During a wonderful visit to the Little River Inn near Mendocino, I had these for breakfast one morning. The hotcakes and the Inn are unforgettable!"

Kathy Warren   **McClatchy High School, Sacramento, CA**

JULE KAGA

Makes 1 round loaf

1 cup milk, scalded
1/2 cup sugar
1 teaspoon salt
1/2 cup shortening
1/4 cup warm water
2 packages yeast

4 1/2 cups flour, sifted & divided
1 1/2 teaspoons cardamom
1/2 cup raisins
1/4 cup citron, chopped
1/4 cup cherries, chopped
1/4 cup almonds. chopped

Frosting:
1 cup powdered sugar
1 tablespoon milk
1/4 teaspoon vanilla

nuts
candied fruit

Scald milk; stir in sugar, salt and shortening. Cool to lukewarm. In a bowl, place warm water, sprinkle in the yeast and stir until dissolved. Stir in the lukewarm milk mixture. Add 2 cups flour and beat thoroughly. Cover and let rise in a warm place, free from draft until doubled in bulk, about 30 minutes. Stir down. Stir in cardamom, raisins, citron, cherries and almonds. Add the remaining 2 1/2 cups flour. Turn out on lightly floured counter. Knead until smooth and elastic. Place in a greased bowl; brush with shortening. Cover and let rise in a warm place, free from draft, until doubled in bulk, about 55 minutes. Punch down. Form into round ball and place on large greased baking sheet. Cover, let rise in warm place, until doubled in size, about 1 hour. Bake at 400 degrees for 10 minutes, then reduce heat to 350 and continue baking for 40 minutes. Cool. Frost with frosting made with 1 cup powdered sugar, 1 tablespoon milk and 1/4 teaspoon vanilla. Combine ingredients for frosting and mix well. Frost the bread. Decorate with nuts and candied fruit.

"Grandma Tompsett's favorite Christmas- time bread our family loves during the holidays."

Sonja Tyree   **Ayala High School, Chino Hills, CA**

SWEDISH RYE BREAD

Makes 3 loaves   **SWEDEN**

1 cake yeast
1/2 cup + 1 tablespoon sugar,
*   divided*
2 1/2 cups warm water, divided
1/4 cup molasses

1 - 2 teaspoons salt
1 tablespoon fennel seed
2 1/2 cups rye flour
2 tablespoons shortening
1/2 cup brown sugar

Dissolve yeast and 1 tablespoon sugar in 1/2 cup warm water; set aside. Mix all remaining ingredients with yeast mixture and blend well, adding small amounts of white flour until dough is soft and pliable. Knead and place in greased bowl. When dough has doubled in size, punch down, turn over and let rise until it is 2 times it's size (about 1 hour). Punch down again and let dough stand 20 minutes. Divide dough into 3 loaves and place in loaf pans. Let rise again until doubled in bulk. Bake in a slow oven, 300 - 325 degrees for 45 minutes.

"My mom's special recipe for all our family holidays and special occasions."

Barbara Bressler   **Buena Park High School, Buena Park, CA**

OLD-FASHIONED FRUIT SOUP

Serves 6 - 8   **SWEDEN**

3/4 cup dried apricots
3/4 cup dried prunes
6 cups cold water
1 cinnamon stick
2 lemon slices, 1/4" thick
3 tablespoons quick-cooking tapioca

1 cup sugar
2 tablespoons raisins
1 tablespoon dried currants
1 tart cooking apple, peeled,
*   cored and cut into 1/2" thick*
*   pieces*

Soak the dried apricots and prunes in cold water for 30 minutes. Since the dried fruit expands considerably as it absorbs the water, you will need at least a 3-quart saucepan. Add the cinnamon stick, lemon slices, tapioca and sugar and bring to a boil. Reduce heat; cover and simmer for 10 minutes, stirring occasionally. Stir in raisins, currants and apple slices and simmer an additional 5 minutes, or until apples are tender. Pour contents of saucepan into a large bowl and let cool to room temperature. Remove the cinnamon stick and cover the bowl with plastic wrap. Set in refrigerator to chill. Serve the fruit soup in compote dishes or soup bowls.

"I first made this recipe when I was in high school (in Home Ec. class) and still enjoy using it."

Karen Beigle   **Villa Park High School, Villa Park, CA**

AGURKESALAT (CUCUMBERS IN VINEGAR)

Serves 6   **DENMARK**

2 large cucumbers   *1 1/2 cups sugar*
3/4 cup vinegar   *salt and pepper to taste*

Peel the cucumbers. Slice as thin as a newspaper. Mix the other ingredients and pour over the cucumbers. May be eaten at once, but flavor will be improved by standing several hours at room temperature, under the pressure of a plastic lid with a weight on top (such as several cans of soup, etc.).

"My grandmother, Nana, would always serve this side salad with her many delicious dinners. My mom, sisters and I fondly remember her salad with the tower of cans on top!"

Shirley Blough   **Hillside Junior High School, Simi Valley, CA**

FRIKADELLER (MEATBALLS W/SALT PORK)

Serves 6   **DENMARK**

1 onion, minced   *1 cup cracker crumbs or dry*
3/4 pound salt pork   *   bread crumbs*
1 pound beef chuck   *salt, to taste*
1 hard-crust roll   *pepper, to taste*
2 cups milk   *1 cup butter*
5 eggs

Mix onion with salt pork and beef which have been ground together by you or your butcher. Soak the hard roll in the milk. Mix with the meats, breaking up the roll to distribute it thoroughly through the meat mixture. Beat 4 eggs and add to meat mixture. Shape into balls. Beat the remaining egg; mix with dry crumbs and coat the meatballs with the mixture. Add salt and pepper to taste to each meat ball. Fry in hot butter, turning frequently to brown all over. Cook until done to taste.

"Serve these with Persillesauce (Parsley Sauce), recipe follows."

Ginny Clark   **Sonora High School, La Habra, CA**

PERSILLESAUCE (PARSLEY SAUCE)

Serves 6   **DENMARK**

2 tablespoons butter   *pepper, to taste*
2 tablespoons flour   *2 tablespoons parsley, minced*
salt, to taste   *1 cup milk*

Melt the butter over low heat. Stir in the flour, salt, pepper and parsley and mix until smooth.
Add the milk gradually, stirring constantly. Allow sauce to cook for 15 minutes at low
temperature, stirring from time to time.

"Serve with Frikadeller (Meatballs w/Salt Pork)."

Ginny Clark   **Sonora High School, La Habra, CA**

SAND BAKKELS

Makes 10-12 doz.   **DUTCH**

1 cup butter   *2 eggs*
1 cup Crisco   *2 teaspoons vanilla*
1 cup sugar   *4 1/2 cups flour*

Cream butter and Crisco; add sugar. Beat eggs slightly and add to creamed mixture. Add
vanilla and flour; mix well. Press into Sand Bakkel or tart tins. The thinner you can press
the dough, the better they turn out. Bake at 450 degrees for 10 to 12 minutes, until a light
golden brown. Turn upside down when done and tap out of tins. Do not wash tins between
bakings.

"This recipe has been handed down from my great grandmother in North Dakota."

Renee Paulsin   **Hemet High School, Hemet, CA**

ALMOND TARTS

Serves 12   **DENMARK**

2/3 cup butter   *1 1/2 cups flour*
1/3 cup sugar   *1/4 teaspoon almond extract*
1 egg yolk
1/2 cup almonds, blanched
*   and ground*

Cream butter and sugar until light and fluffy. Stir in egg yolk and ground almonds. Add flour
and almond extract. Divide dough in half; shape each into a log; divide each into 12 equal
pieces. Press into tiny tart pans, covering the interior 1/4 inch thick. Bake at 325 degrees
for 12 minutes, or until lightly browned. Remove from pans to cool. Fill with sweetened
whipped cream, pudding or fruit filling. Garnish with maraschino cherries or nuts.

*"To remove tart shells from pans easily, cut strips of paper pan liner 1/4 wide.
Place strips across each tart pan before pressing in the dough. Use papers for
removing the shells."*

Mary Lash   **Paramount High School, Paramount, CA**

PEACH PIE

Serves 6 NORWAY

5 fresh peaches, blanched, halved,
*   pits removed*
1 9" pie crust, unbaked

1 cup sugar
1/4 cup flour
1/4 cup margarine

Prepare peaches by blanching in boiling water to remove skins; halve and remove pit. Place peaches, cut side down, into unbaked pie shell. In a bowl, combine sugar, flour and butter or margarine using a pastry blender to cut in; sprinkle mixture over peaches in pie shell. Bake at 400 degrees for 10 minutes; then at 375 degrees for 45 minutes; remove to cool completely. Serve.

"Enjoy a caramelized peach pie that will create your very own aurora borealis to brighten up your next meal as only the Norwegians know how! This is a delicious alternative peach loves won't want to resist - my Norwegian mother's family tradition."

Debbie Sullivan **Silverado High School, Henderson, NV**

SHOO-FLY PIE

Serves 8 DUTCH

1 9" pie crust, unbaked
1 cup flour, sifted
1/2 teaspoon nutmeg
1 teaspoon cinnamon
1/2 cup granulated sugar

1/3 cup butter
1/2 teaspoon baking powder
3/4 cup water
3/4 cup molasses

Combine flour, nutmeg, cinnamon and sugar. Cut in butter to make coarse crumbs. Sprinkle half of the crumbs on bottom of pie shell. Dissolve baking soda in water. Add molasses and mix well. Pour mixture over crumbs. Top with remaining crumbs. Bake at 425 degrees for 15 to 20 minutes, until crust and crumbs are golden brown.

"A family favorite when I was growing up. This pie is not easily found in the West, but is very popular in Pennsylvania. It is called Shoo-Fly because the cook had to shoo the flies away as it cooled."

Adrienne Pringle **Royal High School, Simi Valley, CA**

WHOOPIE PIES

Serves many DUTCH

2 cups sugar
2 eggs
2 teaspoons vanilla
1 cup shortening
2 teaspoons soda
1 cup boiling water

1 cup sour milk
4 cups flour
1 cup cocoa
2 teaspoons salt

Cream sugar, eggs, vanilla and shortening. Combine soda and boiling water. Sift together flour, cocoa and salt. Add milk and soda water to mixture alternating with the flour mixture. Drop by teaspoonfuls onto greased cookie sheet. Bake at 400 degrees for 8 to 20 minutes. Spread filling generously between 2 cookies after they are cooled. Wrap individually in plastic wrap to store. Filling follows.

"These are like big, soft Oreos. This recipe comes form my sister Kathy, whose husband, Clete, is from Pennsylvania."

Shirley Marshman   **West Middle School, Downey, CA**

WHOOPIE PIE FILLING

Serves many   **DUTCH**

2 egg whites	*1/4 cup milk*
2 tablespoons vanilla	*4 cups powdered sugar*
1/4 cup flour	*1 1/2 cups shortening*

Cream egg whites, vanilla, flour, milk and 2 cups powdered sugar. Add 2 more cups sugar and shortening; blend until smooth.

Shirley Marshman   **West Middle School, Downey, CA**

SPECULAAS COOKIES

Makes 20 - 30   **DUTCH**

1 pound butter	*1 teaspoon baking powder*
1 1/2 cups sugar	*1/2 teaspoon salt*
1 1/2 cups brown sugar	*5 cups flour*
2 teaspoons cinnamon	*3 eggs*
2 teaspoons nutmeg	*1 cup walnuts, chopped*
1 teaspoon ground cloves	

Cream together butter, sugar and brown sugar. In a separate bowl, mix cinnamon, nutmeg, cloves, baking powder and salt. Stir the flour into the spices. Beat eggs into butter and sugar mixture, and slowly mix in flour mixture. Stir in the walnuts. Divide the dough into 4 or 5 portions and roll into log shapes; wrap in waxed paper and refrigerate overnight. When ready to bake, slice and bake at 350 degrees for 12 to 15 minutes.

"This recipe came from the Dutch cookbook put out by Hanford Christian School. My mother, Doris Verboon, makes them often for her grandkids to enjoy."

Carole Delap   **Golden West High School, Visalia, CA**

KLETSKOPJES (CHATTER BOXES)

Makes 3 - 4 dozen   **NORWAY**

1/2 cup butter, softened	*1 cup flour, sifted*
1 1/2 cups brown sugar	*1/2 cup almonds, blanched and*
1/8 teaspoon salt	*chopped (2 1/2 ounces)*

In a mixing bowl, combine all ingredients and mix together well. Form into small balls, the size of marbles. Place on an ungreased cookie sheet, approximately 2 1/2 inches apart. Place on lower rack of oven and bake at 400 degrees for 5 minutes or until dough flattens out. Cool and remove with a spatula.

"These cookies are named Chatter Boxes because they crackle and crunch when you eat them."

Susan Lefler   **Ramona Junior High School, Chino, CA**

PEPPARKAKOR

Makes 3 - 4 dozen   **SWEDEN**

3 1/2 cups flour   *1 cup sugar*
2 teaspoons ginger   *1 cup butter or shortening (do NOT*
2 teaspoons cinnamon   *use margarine)*
2 teaspoons cloves   *1 egg*
1 teaspoon baking soda   *1/2 cup molasses*
1/2 teaspoon salt

Sift together dry ingredients; set aside. Cream sugar and butter. Add egg and molasses. Blend in dry ingredients thoroughly. Let dough stand overnight for easy rolling. On a well-floured board, roll out dough to 1/8" thickness. Cut into shapes (we usually make gingerbread people) and bake at 350 degrees for 10 minutes.

"These cookies are made by my mother every Christmas for her VASA club. They are served by St. Lucia on December 13."

Diane Castro   **Quartz Hill High School, Quartz Hill, CA**

BERLINER KRANSER

Makes 4 - 5 dozen   **NORWAY**

4 raw egg yolks   *1 pound butter*
1 cup sugar   *4 egg whites*
4 egg yolks, hard cooked   *sugar, white or loaf (for dipping)*
4 cups flour

Beat yolks of raw eggs with the sugar. Mash the hard cooked yolks and mix. Cream the flour and butter together and mix in with egg mixture. Chill dough. Roll out by hand, into strips, about 1/4" around, cut into 4" lengths. Form into wreaths, laying ends together to form rings. Beat the leftover egg whites until frothy. Dip the wreaths in egg whites, then into white sugar or crushed loaf sugar. Bake at 325 degrees for 5 to 10 minutes.

"The loaf sugar makes these butter cookies a real stand-out on a Christmas cookie platter."

Karen Kegley   **Grant Sawyer Middle School, Las Vegas, NV**

JAN HAGEL

Makes 50 **DUTCH/HOLLAND**

1 cup butter
1 cup sugar
1 egg, separated
2 cups flour

1 teaspoon cinnamon
1 tablespoon water
1/2 cup nuts, finely chopped
   (pecans, almonds or walnuts)

Cream butter and sugar; add egg yolk; beat well. Sift together flour and cinnamon. Stir into butter mixture; mix well. Pat into greased baking pan (15 1/2" x 10 1/2"). Beat egg white with water until frothy. Brush top of cookie mixture; sprinkle with nuts. Bake at 350 degrees for 20 to 25 minutes, until lightly browned. Cut immediately in 3" x 1" squares. Remove from pan to cool.

"Ana Idsinga shared this recipe with our 4-H'ers many years ago."

Mary Lash   **Paramount High School, Paramount, CA**

OLIEBOLLEN

Serves 8 - 10 **DUTCH**

1/2 tablespoon yeast
1 cup lukewarm milk
1 1/2 cup all-purpose flour
1 tablespoon margarine, melted
1 tablespoon sugar
1/2 egg

1 teaspoon salt
1 cup raisins
oil for frying
powdered sugar, for coating
   each oliebol

Dissolve yeast in milk. Combine remaining ingredients. Add yeast-milk mixture to remaining ingredients. Place in a warm place; cover and let rise until it doubles its bulk. Heat oil in electric frying pan to 350 degrees. Drop dough by tablespoonfuls into oil. Fry until golden brown. Drain on paper toweling. Sprinkle with powdered sugar.

"It's a Dutch tradition to serve this on New Year's Eve or New Year's Day."

Astrid Curfman   **Newcomb Academy, Long Beach, CA**

KRUMKAKE

Makes 7 - 8 dozen **NORWAY**

4 eggs, separate
12 ounces evaporated skimmed milk
3/4 cup margarine, melted and cooled

3/4 cup brown sugar
2 teaspoons vanilla
3 cups flour, sifted

Beat egg yolks with a fork. Stir in evaporated milk and melted margarine. Stir in brown sugar and vanilla. Stir in flour, one cup at a time. Beat egg whites until stiff. Fold egg whites into batter. Bake on a krumkake iron until golden brown and immediately roll in a wooden cone to shape.

Becky Oppen   **Dana Hills High School, Dana Point, CA**

ROSETTE COOKIES

Serves many

vegetable oil for deep frying	*1/4 cup milk*
1 egg	*1/2 cup flour*
1 tablespoon sugar	*1/2 cup powdered sugar or*
1/8 teaspoon salt	*cinnamon sugar*
1 tablespoon oil	*Rosette Iron*

Heat oil (about 2") in a small saucepan. Beat egg, sugar and salt in a small bowl. Beat in 1 tablespoon oil, milk and flour until smooth. Heat rosette iron by placing in hot oil for a minute. Tap excess oil off iron. Dip hot iron in to batter just to top edge of iron. Fry until golden brown (about 30 seconds). Immediately remove rosette, invert on paper towel. Dip rosette into sugar mixture or powdered sugar. Heat iron again in hot oil, tap off excess before making each rosette. If iron is not hot enough, batter will not stick.

"I make these almost every Christmas. These are a wonderfully light dessert."

Cindy Quinn   **Dale Junior High School, Anaheim, CA**

ALPHABETIZED CONTRIBUTORS' LIST

AAA

Agee, Vicki, 123
San Marcos HS, San Marcos

Ali-Christie, Robin, 120
Nevada UHS, Grass Valley

Allen, Barbara, 134
Ayala HS, Chino

Alves, Dorothy, 60
Grace Davis HS, Modesto

Anderson, Ramona, 114
Mira Mesa HS, San Diego

Arkus, Phyllis, 35
Lakewood HS, Lakewood

Atkinson, Jennette, 121
Brinley MS, Las Vegas, NV

BBB

Baczynski, Kathie, 51
Mt. Carmel HS, San Diego

Bahn, Adrienne, 59
Lee JHS, Woodland

Bankhead, Marilyn, 32
San Marcos HS, San Marcos

Banks, Judy, 6
Temecula Valley HS, Temecula

Barnard, Cari, 85
Murrieta Valley HS, Murrieta

Bartholomew, Patti, 27
Casa Roble Fundamental HS,
Orangevale

Becker, Trena, 75
Ball JHS, Anaheim

Beigle, Karen, 137
Villa Park HS, Villa Park

Bergmann-Montelongo, Tricia,
67, 95, South JHS, Anaheim

Betz, Judy, 63
Greenfield JHS, Bakersfield

Beutler, Michele, 10
A.B. Miller HS, Fontana

Bleecker, Laurie, 5
Chino HS, Chino

Blohm, Rita, 86
Nogales HS, La Puente

Blough, Shirley, 137
Hillside JHS, Simi Valley

Bowman, Cindy, 83
McFarland HS, McFarland

Bradley, Amber, 120
Granite Hills HS, El Cajon

Brayton, Linda, 14
Grace Davis HS, Modesto

Bressler, Barbara, 136
Buena Park HS, Buena Park

Brown, Darlene, 118
Golden Valley MS,
San Bernardino

Brown, Marjorie, 32
Cabrillo HS, Lompoc

Brown, Susan, 115
Sowers MS, Huntington Beach

Browning, Renee, 30
Hesperia HS, Hesperia

Bruce, Libby, 82
Troy HS, Fullerton

Brunson, Nancy, 81
McKinleyville HS, McKinleyville

Bundy, Betty, 22
Hidden Valley MS, Escondido

Burke, Brenda, 28, 114
Mt. Whitney HS, Visalia

Burkhart, Nanci, 60
Hueneme HS, Oxnard

Burnham, Jill, 68
Bloomington HS, Bloomington

Byrne, Betty, 32
Vaca Pena MS, Vacaville

CCC

California Poultry
Industry Federation, 130

Call, Carole, 20
Costa Mesa HS, Costa Mesa

Campbell, Theresa, 74
John F. Kennedy HS, La Palma

Carlson, Monica, 91
La Contenta JHS, Yucca Valley

Carr, Mary, 113
Enterprise HS, Redding

Carriere, Julie, 16
North Monterey County HS,
Castroville

Castro, Diane, 141
Quartz Hill HS, Quartz Hill

Childers, Penny, 133
Ramona HS, Ramona

Clark, Ginny, 137, 138
Sonora HS, La Habra

Clements, Simon, 71
Bret Harte HS, Altaville

Croce, Angela, 93
Mira Mesa HS, San Diego

Cronkhite, Mary, 135
Antelope Valley HS, Lancaster

Cummings, Carolyn, 2, 99
Newhart MS, Mission Viejo

Curfman, Astrid, 142
Newcomb , Long Beach

Curtis, Pat, 84
Ensign JHS, Newport Beach

DDD

Dallas, Pat, 102
Westminster HS, Westminster

Deeton, Millie, 52
Ayala HS, Chino

Del Monte Foods, 75, 79

Delap, Carole, 58, 140
Golden West HS, Visalia

DellaZoppa, Peg, 46
Yucca Valley HS, Yucca Valley

Demele, Alice, 81, 98
Colton HS, Colton

Drescher, Carol, 26
Camarillo HS, Camarillo

Drewisch, Carrie, 7, 107
Vandenberg MS, Lompoc

Dyle, Patty, 105
Kennedy HS, La Palma

EEE

Easton, Colleen, 81
Brea-Olinda HS, Brea

Escola, Carla, 19
Ripon HS, Ripon

Estes, Marianne, 113
La Mirada HS, La Mirada

Evans, Larkin, 117
Half Moon Bay HS,
Half Moon Bay

FFF

Falkenstien, Linda, 109
Morro Bay HS, Morro Bay

Fecchino, Pam, 52
Cimarron-Memorial HS,
Las Vegas, NV

Fial, Joanne, 89
East MS, Downey

Fincher-Ranger, Beverly, 69
Carpinteria HS, Carpinteria

Fippin, Donna, 40
Bret Harte HS, Altaville

Flath, Maggy, 54
Nevada UHS, Grass Valley

Fleming, Carol, 8
Rancho Cucamonga HS,
Rancho Cucamonga

Ford, Pam, 122
Temecula Valley HS, Temecula

Francois, Cathy, 58
Carlsbad HS, Carlsbad

Francuch, Gloria, 50
Carpinteria HS, Carpinteria

Fregulia, Maria, 65, 67
Lassen UHS, Susanville

Fuller, Glenell, 30
Glendora HS, Glendora

GGG

Garland, Rosemary, 44
Ontario HS, Ontario

Gauthier, Barbara, 84
Santana HS, Santee

Giannetti, Vicki, 65
Foothill HS, Sacramento

Gibbons, Julie, 3
Chemawa MS, Riverside

Goddard, Carol, 12
Alhambra HS, Alhambra

Goedert, Luann, 18
Carlsbad HS, Carlsbad

Goodell, Joan, 16, 99
Eldorado HS, Las Vegas, NV

Goosev, Tanya, 50
Reedley HS, Reedley

Griffith, Janet, 79
Norco HS, Norco

Grohmann, Joyce, 72
Bellflower HS, Bellflower

HHH

Haas, Kristine, 9, 133
La Habra HS, La Habra

Hall, Willy, 85
Orange HS, Orange

Hamilton, Donna, 74
Del Oro HS, Loomis

Hansen, Barbara, 127
Montclair HS, Montclair

Hawkins, Kris, 69
Clovis West HS, Fresno

Haws, Darlene, 23
Highland HS, Bakersfield

Hayes, Sandra, 117
Redlands HS, Redlands

Heinbach, Linda, 21
Yosemite HS, Oakhurst

Heitzmann, Charlotte, 59
Mariposa County HS, Mariposa

Henderson, Gerry, 106
Temple City HS, Temple City

Henry, Chris, 33
Rancho Starbuck JHS, Whittier

Henry, Judy, 28
Mission Viejo HS, Mission Viejo

Herford, Val, 29
Mesa IS, Palmdale

Herndon, Peggy, 41
Central Valley HS, Central Valley

Hershey Foods Corp., 124

Hevener, Judy, 73
Porterville HS, Porterville

Hewes, Gage, 11, 46
South Pasadena HS,
South Pasadena

Hill, Diana F., 70
Sunnymead MS, Moreno Valley

Hirth, Jan, 63
Saddleback HS, Santa Ana

Hoffman, Maria, 13, 33
Katella HS, Anaheim

Holtz, Sheryl, 48, 80
Redwood IS, Thousand Oaks

Hope, Sue, 36
Lompoc HS, Lompoc

Hsieh, Linda, 78
Rowland HS, Rowland Heights

Huckert, Anita, 120
Greenfield JHS, Bakersfield

Huffman, Judith, 9
Mariposa County HS, Mariposa

Hurt, Gail, 64
Estancia HS, Costa Mesa

III

Ikkanda, Reiko, 27, 104
South Pasadena MS,
South Pasadena

Iverson, Katherine, 76
Vandenberg MS, Lompoc

JJJ

Jackson, Carole, 25
Apple Valley HS, Apple Valley

Johnson, Cindy, 42
Orland HS, Orland

Johnson, Wendy, 17
Temecula Valley HS, Temecula

Jones, Dotti, 54
Etiwanda HS,
Rancho Cucamonga

Jones, Dotti, 45
Etiwanda HS,
Rancho Cucamonga

Jones, Pat, 89
Buena HS, Ventura

Jordan, Nancy, 129
Merced HS, Merced

KKK

Kagy, Carol, 34
Norwalk HS, Norwalk

Katen, Mary, 123
Central Valley HS, Central Valley

Kau, Bonnie, 6
Scripps Ranch HS, San Diego

Kaylor, Phyllis, 43
Ray Kroc MS, San Diego

Keema, Susan, 73
Cimarron-Memorial HS,
Las Vegas, NV

Kegley, Karen, 141
Grant Sawyer MS,
Las Vegas, NV

Kile, Mary Ellen, 90
Edison HS, Huntington Beach

King, Gloria, 16
Schurr HS, Montebello

Kolberg-Bentle, Beth, 71
Rancho HS,
North Las Vegas, NV

LLL

Lambert, Gail, 111
El Rancho MS, Anaheim Hills

Landin, Bonnie, 35
Garden Grove HS,
Garden Grove

Lane, Jeri, 8, 10
Canyon Springs HS,
Moreno Valley

Lash, Mary, 138, 142
Paramount HS, Paramount

Lee, Diana, 87
Elsinore MS, Lake Elsinore

Lefler, Susan, 141
Ramona JHS, Chino

Lewandowski, Alice, 17
Linden HS, Linden

Lievre, Helen, 76
La Canada HS, La Canada

Linberger, Kay, 62
Tokay HS, Lodi

Lizardi, Diane, 124
Downey HS, Downey

Love, Donna, 14
Pinon Mesa MS, Phelan

Lucero, Laurie, 85
Santa Maria HS, Santa Maria

Lupul, Darlene, 15, 91
Tokay HS, Lodi

MMM

Malone, Sheryl, 39, 97
Mt. Carmel HS, San Diego

Marshman, Shirley, 140
West MS, Downey

Maurice, Sharron, 47
Blythe MS, Blythe

May, Laura, 94
Hesperia JHS, Hesperia

McAuley, Gail, 62
Lincoln HS, Stockton

McBride, Carolyn, 12
Arcadia HS, Arcadia

McCord, Karen, 92
Lindsay HS, Lindsay

McDaniels, Cheryl, 88, 111
Green Valley HS,
Henderson, NV

McLeod, Margaret, 13
Nogales HS, La Puente

Miller, Cathy, 127
Montclair HS, Montclair

Mills, Ruth Anne, 127
Los Alisos IS, Mission Viejo

Montemagni, Maria, 70
Strathmore HS, Strathmore

Montoy, Joanne, 64
Esperanza HS, Anaheim

Moody, Deanne, 51, 104
Monte Vista HS, Spring Valley

Mornac, Jean, 15
Hillside JHS, Simi Valley

Muraoka, June, 26
Cypress HS, Cypress

NNN

Nadell, Robyn, 48
Bernardo Yorba MS,
Yorba Linda

Nagami, Edna, 46
Carr IS, Santa Ana

National Broiler Council, 40, 54

National Fisheries Institute, 40

National Live Stock and Meat
Board, 14, 31
Chicago, IL

Contributors' List

Skrifvars, Paula, 7
Brea JHS, Brea

Sobey, Teena, 72
Chaparral HS, Las Vegas, NV

Souza, Jane, 109
North Monterey County HS,
Castroville

St. Louis, Lera, 83
Buena HS, Ventura

Stahl, Teresa, 19
Needles Middle/ HS, Needles

Steele, Carol, 112
La Paz IS, Mission Viejo

Street, Carleen, 66
Wasco HS, Wasco

Sullivan, Debbie, 56, 139
Silverado HS, Henderson, NV

Sweet, Connie, 102
Rim of the World HS,
Lake Arrowhead

Sweet-Gregory, Jill, 25
Santa Paula HS, Santa Paula

Swennes, Donna, 119
El Capitan HS, Lakeside

Swift, Beth, 116
Buena Park HS, Buena Park

TTT

Talley, Karen, 56
Santa Maria HS, Santa Maria

Tam, Marilyn, 61
Orange Glen HS, Escondido

Thomas, Dale, 83
Mira Mesa HS, San Diego

Thomas, Denise, 103
Matilija JHS, Ojai

Thomas, Evelyn, 8
Chaffey HS, Ontario

Tilson, Karen, 95, 106
Poly HS, Riverside

Tingley, Janet, 116
Atascadero HS, Atascadero

Tomlinson, Judy, 77
Colusa HS, Colusa

Topp, Judi, 119
A.B.Miller HS, Fontana

Traw, Marianne, 59
Ball JHS, Anaheim

Turner, Sharon, 65
El Dorado HS, Placentia

Tyree, Sonja, 93, 136
Ayala HS, Chino Hills

UUU

Umbro, Brenda, 69
Orange Glen HS, Escondido

WWW

Walters, Sue, 100
Morse HS, San Diego

Walther, Sheryal, 130, 131
Lakewood HS, Lakewood

Ward, Elizabeth, 113
Norte Vista HS, Riverside

Warren, Barbara, 53
Colton HS, Colton

Warren, Kathy, 135
McClatchy HS, Sacramento

Waterbury, Sue, 31
San Luis Obispo HS,
San Luis Obispo

Waugh, Lynda, 60
San Marcos JHS, San Marcos

Weiss, Deborah, 36
Ayala HS, Chino

Wells, Betty, 94
Oroville HS, Oroville

Westmoreland, Myrna, 7
Grace Davis HS, Modesto

White, Laury, 57
Baldwin Park HS,
Baldwin Park

Wilfert, Lorna, 122
Huntington Beach HS,
Huntington Beach

Williams, Liz, 112
Ontario HS, Ontario

Wisconsin Milk Marketing
Board, 110

Woll, Jeanette, 105, 107
Antelope Valley HS,
Antelope Valley

Wong, Pat, 43
Taft HS, Taft

Woolley, Linda, 38
La Sierra HS, Riverside

YYY

Yonehara, Sharon F., 28
Big Valley HS, Beiber

ZZZ

Zallar, Sue, 37
Capistrano Valley HS,
 San Juan Capistrano

INDEX OF RECIPES BY CATEGORY

           Index by Category

DESSERTS

SALADS

SOUPS

VEGETABLES/SIDE DISHES

- - - - - - - - - - - - - - - -

WORLD WIDE RECIPES

California Cookbook Company

1907 Skycrest Drive

Fullerton, CA 92631

Please send ___ copy(ies) of your cookbook at **$9.95** each (includes tax and postage). Make checks payable to: *California Cookbook Company.*

Enclosed is my check for $ _____

Name _____

Street _____

City _____ State _____ Zip _____

- - - - - - - - - - - - - - - -

WORLD WIDE RECIPES

California Cookbook Company

1907 Skycrest Drive

Fullerton, CA 92631

Please send ___ copy(ies) of your cookbook at **$9.95** each (includes tax and postage). Make checks payable to: *California Cookbook Company.*

Enclosed is my check for $ _____

Name _____

Street _____

City _____ State _____ Zip _____

INDEX OF RECIPES BY COUNTRY